New Beginnings

Other books by this Author:
Be Transformed: By the Spirit of the Living God 2011

The sequel to this book is entitled *Fishers of Men: Becoming a Dynamic Disciple of Jesus Christ,* and is scheduled to be released in 2018. *Fishers of Men* takes the Christian to the next level of knowledge and equips one for greater service to God. *Be Transformed* has been used successfully in many different denominations. It works well for women's and men's groups, as well as individual studies. It has changed countless lives.

Be Transformed Ministries was founded in 2011, after the publication of Sharon's first book, Be Transformed: By the Spirit of the Living God. The mission of the ministry is to share the Gospel of Jesus Christ through speaking engagements, teaching in small groups, continued publishing, and a brochure ministry to reach the lost. A significant part of Be Transformed Ministries is to reach those in prisons, jails, and rehabs by sending thousands of our books to the facilities at no cost to them. As of 2017, Be Transformed books are in 40 different institutions around the United States, with over 900 copies distributed into the Los Angeles County Jail.

Visit our website to learn more about Be Transformed Ministries, or to purchase our books. You can also learn about how you can partner with us financially and prayerfully at: **betransformedministries.com**

Follow us on facebook at: **facebook.com/betransformedministries**
Email us at: **betransformed@betransformedministries.com**
Snail mail is P.O. Box 597, Grover Beach, CA 93458
Thank you!

New Beginnings

Understanding the Basic Principles of the Christian Faith

Group or Individual Study

Scriptures Included

By
Sharon Dutra

DEDICATION

I would like to dedicate this book to all of the men and women I have had the privilege of teaching over the years.

You stood by me as I was learning to teach. You loved me and encouraged me, even when I was a hard taskmaster at times. You were patient and steadfast in your commitment to our Bible studies.

You have continually inspired me to reach my highest potential – to be the best teacher and author I could possibly become, by the grace of God.

None of this work would have been possible without you. I thank you with all of my heart.

A special thanks to all of those who spent countless hours studying, editing and proofreading my work.

To Michael, my husband, you are God's greatest gift to me.

And of course, my life would be in total shambles without the redeeming work and love of Jesus Christ, my Lord and Savior. My greatest desire is to love You fully and devote my entire life and effort to You, my Jesus.

ABOUT THE AUTHOR

Sharon Dutra was once a homeless drug addict who hated her life. She tried to commit suicide several times. During her incarceration, she accepted Jesus Christ into her life, and she has never been the same.

God has gifted her in teaching and evangelism, and her books are the fruit of these gifts. Sharon's greatest desire is to win people to Christ and to equip them to become dynamic disciples of Jesus Christ. This book is simple and straightforward, and will help Christians learn the foundational tenets of faith from the Bible.

"It's not easy confronting the unpleasant things in life. But Sharon Dutra does just that. She not only tackles them, but she puts on the full armor of God and goes to battle with you and beside you in your faith. She equips you with the tools you need along the way. I have become a much more victorious Christian in my everyday life because of Sharon's teaching. She is a gifted writer who is led by the Holy Spirit in hopes of bringing peace and serenity to the lives of others. She helps you confront some of life's toughest issues. Her testimony brings hope; her teaching and writing brings change; and her charismatic and transparent love for God brings inspiration to those who choose to believe in Jesus Christ. Sharon invests her heart and soul, along with insight, into her writing. She simplifies her books in a way that make them teachable, applicable, and life-changing. The ultimate goal and desire of her heart is to help others "be transformed" in their daily walk with Christ. We have sat under Sharon's teaching for a year and a half, and are here to testify that many areas of our lives have been transformed, as well. We would like to say thank you, Sharon, for sharing your life-changing gift with us. We pray your light for Jesus continues to shine through your future writing and through your ministry. Many blessings as you move forward. Onward Christian soldier! With grateful hearts and mended souls," *Michael and Susan Guinn, San Luis Obispo, CA*

"Once His earthly ministry was complete, just before He ascended into heaven, Jesus gave His followers this command: "Make disciples of all the nations, and teach these new disciples to obey all the commands I have given you".

With this in mind, Sharon Dutra has written a "back to basics" Bible study to help new or returning disciples grow in their walk with Jesus. This is a great tool for those of us who love to see new believers mature into full-blown disciples of Jesus Christ".

Ron Dee, Associate Pastor
Harvest Church
Arroyo Grande, CA

HOW TO USE THIS BOOK

This book is excellent for group or individual study. The group method that has worked best for us is to have each person in the room take turns reading a paragraph, and look up all the Scriptures as they appear in the text.

There are additional subjects that could have been added to this book, but I selected these chapters in order to facilitate a 12 week Bible study. We usually spend about an hour and 45 minutes for each class. These studies are lengthy and contain many Scriptures, so you probably won't have much time for group discussion. However, if you would like to include more discussion, you may want to extend your 12-week study.

The New Living Translation Bible was used for *New Beginnings*. Ordinarily, I would prefer that students look up the verses in their own Bible so they can become familiar as to where the books and passages are located. However, since this is a book of basic truths, there may be people who are studying the Scriptures for the first time, and looking up the verses would be too time consuming.

For this reason, all of the Scriptures are listed at the back of each chapter. For example, if you turn to the end of Chapter 1, you'll see the heading "Chapter 1, *Scripture Verses*". There is a bold number on the left side of the page. This number corresponds with the "little" number at the end of each Scripture verse in the text, such as Romans 12:2[1]. The number 1 correlates with the number "1" Scripture at the end of the chapter.

PLEASE read all the Scriptures! The Bible is the power behind these studies. You will learn a great deal about God and His ways if you take the time to read them. If you skip reading the Scriptures, you will miss the best part of the book!

My desire is for everyone to learn their Bibles well. You'll learn in the chapter entitled "What is the Bible?" that the daily practice of studying the Word of God is one of the most essential aspects of the Christian life.

You will develop your own method as you facilitate your group, but if you begin as suggested, it will help you to find what works best for your individual setting.

CONTENTS

SIN

What do you think of when you hear the word "sin"? Do you believe that people are bad and that's why they do evil things? Maybe you think most people are good, but they just get caught in bad circumstances that "make them" do terrible things? Or, is it possible we are all born with sin in our nature, and we can't help our wickedness – we can't help but "sin"?

What IS Sin?

The original meaning of sin can be explained as "Missing the Mark" – a term that is used in archery. We all know that hitting the "bulls eye" is the perfect score. This analogy relates to the story of when God created Adam and Eve. God intended for them to live in *perfect* union with Him, doing His *perfect* will and having *perfect* intimacy with Him. There were no barriers of guilt, shame, evil, pride, greed, selfishness – or the resulting punishment. But most of us know the story – Eve bit the apple and invited Adam to share in her disobedience (Genesis 3:1-19[1]). The tragic result of sin is "separation from God". If you have lived apart from God, this separation may not seem like a big deal. However, God is the Giver of all good things, and His absence means the loss of love, joy, peace, and hope in our lives. This is why we feel so empty, lonely, and purposeless at times.

Ever since sin entered the human race through Adam and Eve, all human beings are spiritually alienated from God at birth. This division remains in our lives until we make a conscious decision to surrender to God. We cannot help ourselves out of this condition, because our inborn nature is self-seeking and self-serving, and we believe ourselves to be self-sufficient. But we find that "SELF" is the root of all of our problems (Jeremiah 17:9[2])!

Indeed, the Bible says that our spirits are literally **dead** before we invite Jesus into our hearts (Ephesians 2:1-3[3]; Colossians 2:13[4]). This may be hard to believe, because we've seen those who *appear* to be happy without Him. They may even say they are "spiritual people". However, God says the only authentic way we can be spiritually alive is if Jesus, by His Holy Spirit, is living inside of us.

Another reason the sin nature that we are born with alienates us from God is because He cannot tolerate sin in His presence. And to make things worse, there is no way we can pay for our sin. We can't even try to be "good enough" to be in relationship with God without His intervention. He is absolutely holy, and we just aren't able to work hard enough to satisfy His perfect moral standards (Romans 3:10[5]; 1 Peter 1:15[6]).

The truth is, we are completely incapable of overcoming sin on our own (Romans 5:1-21[7]; 7:14 to 8:8[8]; 1 John 3:4-10[9]). If you don't believe this, just look around at our world. Addiction, greed, hatred, murder, lying, fear, and anger are rampant. Or just watch any 2 year old. They are not taught to be selfish or defiant. It just comes "naturally"! And what about all the times *you* have told yourself "I'm never going to do that again!", but you return to the very behavior or attitude that disgusts you? These are perfect examples of human nature – the *sin* nature - at its core.

Even people we think are "nice" are not free of sin. John 16:9 tells us that the greatest sin of all is refusing to believe in Jesus, who is God Himself. This is because Jesus is "The Way, The Truth, and The Life", and no one can come to God the Father without Him (John 14:6[10]).

Sin is a ferocious enemy and it will always conquer you if you do not subdue it (Genesis 4:7[11]; 2 Peter 2:19[12]).That's the reason we never find *real* peace or satisfaction when we try satisfying ourselves by chasing money, status, sex, power, fame, cravings or possessions. Striving to serve *ourselves* will always produce an emptiness in our souls, because we were *created* to find joy and fulfillment by living in an intimate relationship with God, loving Him and serving Him.

Unfortunately, most of the world will never come to faith in Christ. It is a costly decision, and He requires our full allegiance. Living for Jesus will encompass every aspect of our lives – our mind, our desires, our will, our emotions, our body, our choices, our finances, and our future.

I Didn't Do It!

One of the greatest obstacles in choosing to live life in Christ is that we want to minimize the responsibility for our sin. Most of us have trouble admitting when we are wrong, and it's even more difficult to change our behavior when we *are* wrong. And we must realize that just because we don't commit the "big" sins, such as lying, murder, sexual promiscuity, or stealing, it doesn't mean we are free from sin. There are plenty of transgressions lurking in our hearts, such as gossip, fear, hatred, bigotry, selfishness, rudeness, pride, and the like.

Additionally, the Bible tells us that other forms of sin are "knowing what is right and not doing it", and "knowing something is wrong and doing it anyways" (James 4:17[13]; Romans 14:23[14]). Our sinful condition can pretty well be summed up in 1 John 2:15-17[15].

Whether we admit it or not, we are in desperate need of forgiveness from God and others. This is an essential component to living in healthy relationships. We instinctively know that there is good and evil, right and wrong, and that we need to be pardoned for the things we have done. Forgiveness brings peace to our hearts by removing the barrier of guilt and shame that exists between ourselves, others, and God. In our next chapter, we will discuss the subject of repentance, which describes our decision to turn our focus from "self" and deliberately place our lives in God's hands.

Our Choice Determines Our Eternity

Some people believe that God is mean and angry, and He is just waiting to "zap" us when we sin. But this is a lie. He loves us and wants nothing more than to be in a close relationship with us. What most people fail to understand is that God isn't the one who "sends people to hell". They go to hell because *they refuse* to submit their lives to Him (Romans 1:18-25[16]).

The truth is, God's arms are open wide, ready to receive those who are sorry for their sins and choose to love Him (Isaiah 65:1-2[17]). It is imperative for us to know that it is entirely our choice as to where we will spend eternity. The sin in us will *always* oppose everything God stands for. But we have a Savior who came for the very purpose of setting us free from our sin.

Jesus took our sin, guilt, and shame upon Himself when He died on the cross. But make no mistake - while He is fully love, He is also fully just. He adores us, but He will not overlook sin. If we choose to reject Him, it is at our eternal peril.

Again, it is **our** choice as to where we spend eternity. There will come a day when we all will face our Creator and give an account for the way we have lived (Romans 14:11-12[18]).

Choose Him now while you still have breath.

If you haven't already asked Jesus into your life, or if you have known Him previously and now live apart from Him, you can use this prayer as a guide to ask Him to become the Lord of your life. "Lord" is one of the titles used for Jesus, and it encompasses a loving friend *and* a respected master. He must hold both of these positions in your relationship with Him.

Dear Jesus,
I know I have purposefully rejected You. I have chosen to live life on my terms, making choices that I know are contrary to Your ways, which I now know is sin. And I realize these choices have left me lonely, angry, empty, and dissatisfied. I ask for Your forgiveness now. I want to be filled with joy, peace, and hope, and I believe that You alone are the One to offer me genuine life. So I ask You to please come into my heart and fill me with Your Spirit. Help me to be willing to leave my old life behind and embrace the new life that You have planned for me. I choose to follow You with my whole being, even when I don't understand all that You are doing. I commit to seeking You in Your Bible and in prayer, and finding a Bible-based church so I am able to grow in my new faith. In Jesus Name, Amen.

Turn from your sin today to receive God's forgiveness,
and the power to live a new life!

CHAPTER 1
Scripture Verses

1. **Genesis 3:1-19:** The serpent was the shrewdest of all the wild animals the Lord God had made. One day he asked the woman, "Did God really say you must not eat the fruit from any of the trees in the garden?" ² "Of course we may eat fruit from the trees in the garden," the woman replied. ³ "It's only the fruit from the tree in the middle of the garden that we are not allowed to eat. God said, 'You must not eat it or even touch it; if you do, you will die.'" ⁴ "You won't die!" the serpent replied to the woman. ⁵ "God knows that your eyes will be opened as soon as you eat it, and you will be like God, knowing both good and evil." ⁶ The woman was convinced. She saw that the tree was beautiful and its fruit looked delicious, and she wanted the wisdom it would give her. So she took some of the fruit and ate it. Then she gave some to her husband, who was with her, and he ate it, too. ⁷ At that moment their eyes were opened, and they suddenly felt shame at their nakedness. So they sewed fig leaves together to cover themselves. ⁸ When the cool evening breezes were blowing, the man and his wife heard the Lord God walking about in the garden. So they hid from the Lord God among the trees. ⁹ Then the Lord God called to the man, "Where are you?" ¹⁰ He replied, "I heard you walking in the garden, so I hid. I was afraid because I was naked." ¹¹ "Who told you that you were naked?" the Lord God asked. "Have you eaten from the tree whose fruit I commanded you not to eat?" ¹² The man replied, "It was the woman you gave me who gave me the fruit, and I ate it." ¹³ Then the Lord God asked the woman, "What have you done?" "The serpent deceived me," she replied. "That's why I ate it." ¹⁴ Then the Lord God said to the serpent, "Because you have done this, you are cursed more than all animals, domestic and wild. You will crawl on your belly, groveling in the dust as long as you live. ¹⁵ And I will cause hostility between you and the woman, and between your offspring and her offspring. He will strike your head, and you will strike his

heel." [16] Then he said to the woman, "I will sharpen the pain of your pregnancy, and in pain you will give birth. And you will desire to control your husband, but he will rule over you." [17] And to the man he said, "Since you listened to your wife and ate from the tree whose fruit I commanded you not to eat, the ground is cursed because of you. All your life you will struggle to scratch a living from it. [18] It will grow thorns and thistles for you, though you will eat of its grains. [19] By the sweat of your brow will you have food to eat until you return to the ground from which you were made. For you were made from dust, and to dust you will return."

2. **Jeremiah 17:9:** The human heart is the most deceitful of all things, and desperately wicked. Who really knows how bad it is?

3. **Ephesians 2:1-3:** Once you were dead because of your disobedience and your many sins. [2] You used to live in sin, just like the rest of the world, obeying the devil—the commander of the powers in the unseen world. He is the spirit at work in the hearts of those who refuse to obey God. [3] All of us used to live that way, following the passionate desires and inclinations of our sinful nature. By our very nature we were subject to God's anger, just like everyone else.

4. **Colossians 2:13:** You were dead because of your sins and because your sinful nature was not yet cut away. Then God made you alive with Christ, for he forgave all our sins.

5. **Romans 3:10:** As the Scriptures say, "No one is righteous— not even one."

6. **1 Peter 1:15:** But now you must be holy in everything you do, just as God who chose you is holy.

7. **Romans 5:1-21:** Therefore, since we have been made right in God's sight by faith, we have peace with God because of what Jesus Christ our Lord has done for us. [2] Because of our faith, Christ has brought us into this place of undeserved privilege where we now stand, and we confidently and joyfully look forward to sharing God's glory. [3] We

can rejoice, too, when we run into problems and trials, for we know that they help us develop endurance. [4] And endurance develops strength of character, and character strengthens our confident hope of salvation. [5] And this hope will not lead to disappointment. For we know how dearly God loves us, because he has given us the Holy Spirit to fill our hearts with his love. [6] When we were utterly helpless, Christ came at just the right time and died for us sinners. [7] Now, most people would not be willing to die for an upright person, though someone might perhaps be willing to die for a person who is especially good. [8] But God showed his great love for us by sending Christ to die for us while we were still sinners. [9] And since we have been made right in God's sight by the blood of Christ, he will certainly save us from God's condemnation. [10] For since our friendship with God was restored by the death of his Son while we were still his enemies, we will certainly be saved through the life of his Son. [11] So now we can rejoice in our wonderful new relationship with God because our Lord Jesus Christ has made us friends of God.

[12] When Adam sinned, sin entered the world. Adam's sin brought death, so death spread to everyone, for everyone sinned. [13] Yes, people sinned even before the law was given. But it was not counted as sin because there was not yet any law to break. [14] Still, everyone died—from the time of Adam to the time of Moses—even those who did not disobey an explicit commandment of God, as Adam did. Now Adam is a symbol, a representation of Christ, who was yet to come. [15] But there is a great difference between Adam's sin and God's gracious gift. For the sin of this one man, Adam, brought death to many. But even greater is God's wonderful grace and his gift of forgiveness to many through this other man, Jesus Christ. [16] And the result of God's gracious gift is very different from the result of that one man's sin. For Adam's sin led to condemnation, but God's free gift leads to our being made right with God, even though we are guilty of many sins. [17] For the sin of this one man, Adam, caused death to rule over many. But even greater is God's wonderful grace

and his gift of righteousness, for all who receive it will live in triumph over sin and death through this one man, Jesus Christ. [18] Yes, Adam's one sin brings condemnation for everyone, but Christ's one act of righteousness brings a right relationship with God and new life for everyone. [19] Because one person disobeyed God, many became sinners. But because one other person obeyed God, many will be made righteous.

[20] God's law was given so that all people could see how sinful they were. But as people sinned more and more, God's wonderful grace became more abundant. [21] So just as sin ruled over all people and brought them to death, now God's wonderful grace rules instead, giving us right standing with God and resulting in eternal life through Jesus Christ our Lord.

8. **Romans 7:14-8:8:** [14] So the trouble is not with the law, for it is spiritual and good. The trouble is with me, for I am all too human, a slave to sin. [15] I don't really understand myself, for I want to do what is right, but I don't do it. Instead, I do what I hate. [16] But if I know that what I am doing is wrong, this shows that I agree that the law is good. [17] So I am not the one doing wrong; it is sin living in me that does it. [18] And I know that nothing good lives in me, that is, in my sinful nature. I want to do what is right, but I can't. [19] I want to do what is good, but I don't. I don't want to do what is wrong, but I do it anyway. [20] But if I do what I don't want to do, I am not really the one doing wrong; it is sin living in me that does it.

[21] I have discovered this principle of life—that when I want to do what is right, I inevitably do what is wrong. [22] I love God's law with all my heart. [23] But there is another power within me that is at war with my mind. This power makes me a slave to the sin that is still within me. [24] Oh, what a miserable person I am! Who will free me from this life that is dominated by sin and death? [25] Thank God! The answer is in Jesus Christ our Lord. So you see how it is: In my mind

I really want to obey God's law, but because of my sinful nature I am a slave to sin.

8 So now there is no condemnation for those who belong to Christ Jesus. [2] And because you belong to him, the power of the life-giving Spirit has freed you from the power of sin that leads to death. [3] The law of Moses was unable to save us because of the weakness of our sinful nature. So God did what the law could not do. He sent his own Son in a body like the bodies we sinners have. And in that body God declared an end to sin's control over us by giving his Son as a sacrifice for our sins. [4] He did this so that the just requirement of the law would be fully satisfied for us, who no longer follow our sinful nature but instead follow the Spirit. [5] Those who are dominated by the sinful nature think about sinful things, but those who are controlled by the Holy Spirit think about things that please the Spirit. [6] So letting your sinful nature control your mind leads to death. But letting the Spirit control your mind leads to life and peace. [7] For the sinful nature is always hostile to God. It never did obey God's laws, and it never will. [8] That's why those who are still under the control of their sinful nature can never please God.

9. **1 John 3:4-10:** Everyone who sins is breaking God's law, for all sin is contrary to the law of God. [5] And you know that Jesus came to take away our sins, and there is no sin in him. [6] Anyone who continues to live in him will not sin. But anyone who keeps on sinning does not know him or understand who he is. [7] Dear children, don't let anyone deceive you about this: When people do what is right, it shows that they are righteous, even as Christ is righteous. [8] But when people keep on sinning, it shows that they belong to the devil, who has been sinning since the beginning. But the Son of God came to destroy the works of the devil. [9] Those who have been born into God's family do not make a practice of sinning, because God's life is in them. So they can't keep on sinning, because they are children of God. [10] So now we can tell who are children of God and who are children of the

devil. Anyone who does not live righteously and does not love other believers does not belong to God.

10. **John 14:6:** Jesus told him, "I am the way, the truth, and the life. No one can come to the Father except through me."

11. **Genesis 4:7:** You will be accepted if you do what is right. But if you refuse to do what is right, then watch out! Sin is crouching at the door, eager to control you. But you must subdue it and be its master.

12. **2 Peter 2:19:** They promise freedom, but they themselves are slaves of sin and corruption. For you are a slave to whatever controls you.

13. **James 4:17:** Remember, it is sin to know what you ought to do and then not do it.

14. **Romans 14:23:** But if you have doubts about whether or not you should eat something, you are sinning if you go ahead and do it. For you are not following your convictions. If you do anything you believe is not right, you are sinning.

15. **1 John 2:15-17:** Do not love this world nor the things it offers you, for when you love the world, you do not have the love of the Father in you. [16] For the world offers only a craving for physical pleasure, a craving for everything we see, and pride in our achievements and possessions. These are not from the Father, but are from this world. [17] And this world is fading away, along with everything that people crave. But anyone who does what pleases God will live forever.

16. **Romans 1:18-25:** But God shows his anger from heaven against all sinful, wicked people who suppress the truth by their wickedness. [19] They know the truth about God because he has made it obvious to them. [20] For ever since the world was created, people have seen the earth and sky. Through everything God made, they can clearly see his invisible qualities—his eternal power and divine nature. So they have no excuse for not knowing God. [21] Yes, they knew God, but they wouldn't worship him as God or even give him thanks. And they began to think up foolish ideas of what God was like. As a result,

their minds became dark and confused. [22] Claiming to be wise, they instead became utter fools. [23] And instead of worshiping the glorious, ever-living God, they worshiped idols made to look like mere people and birds and animals and reptiles. [24] So God abandoned them to do whatever shameful things their hearts desired. As a result, they did vile and degrading things with each other's bodies. [25] They traded the truth about God for a lie. So they worshiped and served the things God created instead of the Creator himself, who is worthy of eternal praise! Amen.

17. **Isaiah 65:1-2:** The Lord says, "I was ready to respond, but no one asked for help. I was ready to be found, but no one was looking for me. I said, 'Here I am, here I am!' to a nation that did not call on my name. [2] All day long I opened my arms to a rebellious people. But they follow their own evil paths and their own crooked schemes."

18. **Romans 14:11-12:** For the Scriptures say, "'As surely as I live,' says the LORD, 'every knee will bend to me, and every tongue will declare allegiance to God.'" [12] Yes, each of us will give a personal account to God.

REPENTANCE

There are many people who run from the whole idea of having a relationship with God. They spend their entire lives trying *everything* possible to be 'happy and fulfilled', but they foolishly and purposefully resist the ONE person who can really bring them deep and lasting joy!

The true meaning of repentance is frequently misunderstood. Some folks believe they are too good to bow their knee to anyone. Many cringe at the thought of turning their life around, because it sounds like something that will cut them off from all their fun and pleasure. But the truth is, it is by repentance that we gain our freedom, and how we receive true peace and joy. It is the method by which we decide to renounce our old behavior and embrace the new life that God offers. It is the act of turning *away* from sin and turning *to* Jesus.

I believe there are 3 essential stages we need to go through in order to experience true repentance and become intimate with our Savior. They are: Faith, Humility, and Surrender. There is a more in-depth chapter about Faith in this book, but I have used the topic here to explain its necessity in the path of repentance.

Faith

Faith – which is our belief in God – is what commences this beautiful relationship with our Creator. We must first *believe* that He exists, because everything that follows is hinged on this belief. But it doesn't just stop with our *mental belief* in Him; we need to take the next step by willfully allowing Him to govern our lives (Ephesians 4:20-24[1]).

Simply acknowledging that "God is out there somewhere" is not real faith. The Bible says "Even the demons believe (*that God exists*), and they tremble *in terror*" (James 2:19[2]; *italics mine*). Genuine faith is a gift from God, and this kind of faith transforms our "belief" into an **active decision** to trust God and to move towards a relationship with Him.

Authentic faith is like a living organism. It continues to make necessary and purposeful changes in order to grow. No matter how frightening this new journey may seem, *real faith* will make the determination to begin a lifelong search for a deeper union with God through Jesus Christ.

Humility

Humility is required in order for us to repent. Humility is really just admitting that God is the only perfect Being in the universe, and that we cannot successfully run our lives the way He has intended for us without His help. We find that the opposite of humility is **rebellion**. When we live in sin, we do not display humility. We are essentially saying "I am going to do life *my* way".

When we choose to live in rebellion towards God, we are actually full of **pride**. And when we are dominated by pride – which *leads* to disobedience to God - we don't welcome advice or have any desire to change our ways (2 Corinthians 7:10[3]). We refuse to bend our wills to anyone, even the Almighty. But it is impossible to live for Christ without humility, because we will continually fight Him for the "power seat" in our lives. This will destroy any intimacy or growth we may hope to gain.

Surrender

People are often afraid to surrender to God, because they are unwilling to 'give up' ungodly behaviors in their lives. At some level, people instinctively know there will be some changes that will have to be made if they become accountable to God. This can be frightening, because entering into a relationship with God means giving control of our lives over to someone other than ourselves.

Ironically, we often stay in the same old rut, regardless of how ugly or dysfunctional our lives become. Sometimes, it just "seems" safer to remain in our chaos than to leave our old life behind and embrace the new life that Jesus offers. It's the same principle as to why people stay in abusive relationships or toxic environments – they are driven by their fear.

Others avoid becoming intimate with God because they think becoming a Christian will be boring, or they will be labeled 'weird' or 'intolerant'. Or they witness someone who *says* they are a Christian, but the Christian acts so ungodly that the unbeliever mistakenly believes "Christianity doesn't work". Tragically, these hypocrites cause unbelievers to think Jesus is weak and worthless. Another common reason people avoid God is because they have been hurt by Christians, or have experienced Church to be irrelevant or sterile.

However, I believe the most accurate reason people reject Jesus Christ is that He IS Truth. Therefore, they will *face truth* as they become more intimate with Him. This can be terrifying, because they do not want to see *themselves* truthfully and honestly. They fear they may not like what they see if they examine themselves carefully. Fear is probably the greatest reason why people reject God and His people.

Let's face it: we have all been through the suffering and negative consequences that arise from living by our own rules (Galatians 5:16-17[4], 19-21[5]). The good news is, we often find that our search for God begins when we feel dissatisfied, empty, sorrowful, guilt-ridden, or out of control. Something is telling us there is more to life, and we know deep down that we are missing whatever it is.

Truly surrendering ourselves to God will change our hearts, minds, and lifestyles, so that we reflect more of the character of Jesus as outlined in 1 Corinthians 13:4-7[6] and Galatians 5:22-24[7]. God says that if we truly desire Him and search for Him, *He will be found* (Deuteronomy 4:29[8]). Experiencing intimacy with God brings us the life, the fullness, the purpose, the joy, and the peace our souls have always longed for.

We have all seen the results in our lives when we are controlled by our own selfish choices. If we are honest, we will admit that we cannot help but make decisions that clash with God's will. And unhappiness is always the fruit we bear when we live apart from Him. So the question is: "How many times do we have to find ourselves buried in shame, misery, loneliness, or pain – before we submit to the God who loves us?"

On To Repentance

Repentance actually means "to turn 180 degrees". In fact, it was used in the military when soldiers performed an about-face – they marched in one direction and then turned around so they were moving in the opposite direction. In spiritual terms, repentance is also a "turning around", both in an attitude of our heart, and in our actions. We turn *from* sin – and *to* God.

In order to accept Jesus into our hearts and have Him change our lives, we must accept the fact that we are sinners, and feel sorrowful for the way we have lived apart from Him (Isaiah 57:15[9]; Matthew 4:17[10]; Acts 2:38[11]; 20:21[12]). That is the "heart" of repentance. We must also recognize that when we are living without Christ, we are headed for eternal hopelessness.

Repentance is not only the crucial process by which we initially come to know God, but it needs to become a continual practice in our Christian life. Sorrowfully admitting our shortcomings should always follow our sinful actions. Confessing our sin and turning away from it is the "action" of repentance. Repentance is so beautiful, because it has the ability to cleanse our souls and restore our relationship with God and others.

Another amazing truth about repentance is that when we genuinely accept Jesus' payment for our sin, He is quick to forgive us. Many people have great trouble believing this, thinking they have to continue "paying" for the sin they have committed. However, this is basically implying that Jesus didn't "do enough" to pay for our sins – that He "needs our help". While we *will* have to face the natural consequences for our sin, and make an effort to avoid it in the future, GOD forgives fully when we come to Him in true repentance.

Obviously, we *will* make mistakes, because we aren't perfect. But our sin should be an occasional occurrence, not a habit. If we learn the practice of repenting well, this will keep our hearts soft and teachable. We will then find rest for our souls through God's forgiveness every time we stumble (1 John 1:9-10[13]). Verse 10 in this passage is speaking of "hardening our hearts" – which can happen if we repeatedly refuse to repent and turn back to God's ways. His forgiveness should never be an excuse to do whatever we want, thereby taking His goodness lightly.

Do Something!

When we choose Christ as our Master, we begin to change direction from our old lifestyle and towards God. We start to make choices that please Him, instead of selfishly pleasing ourselves. And this is when we will experience the *abundant life* Jesus offers.

However, we can only do this by the power of the Holy Spirit, who is also God. Trying to live the Christian life without the Spirit always results in *religion* – which is actually meaningless enslavement. We will learn more about the Holy Spirit in a later lesson.

As in any relationship, both sides must put forth effort in order to have a vital connection. God has already proven His love for us through Jesus' death on the cross. Now, it is our responsibility to do everything in our power to stay close to the Lord and make Him our new priority (Matthew 6:33[14]).

As we actively pursue Christ, He will continue to walk by our side and give us the strength and direction we need to do His will. In fact, He delights in doing this (2 Samuel 22:20[15]; Psalm 18:19[16]; 37:23[17])! A beautiful picture of our "before and after" life is found in Isaiah 62:4[18]. No longer will you be desolate (lonely, despairing and empty), but you will be God's very own beloved treasure (Deuteronomy 14:2[19]; 26:18[20]).

The more we bend our will to the Savior, the more like Him we will become. Sharing and confessing our shortcomings and failures with God is an essential component to growing and living in a rewarding Christian life. Jesus doesn't promise that it will be easy to consistently follow Him. He may not change our circumstances, but He promises to be with us *through* them. The pleasure of knowing Him and serving Him is surely the most satisfying and exciting life you can imagine!

We will grow closer to the Lord as we regularly repent. And through attending church, reading the Bible, prayer, and spending time with others who genuinely live out Christian values, our thoughts and actions will become more aligned with God's will.

This new way of living will not come automatically, nor will it happen quickly! It takes time and effort to develop new attitudes and patterns of living. But remember, Jesus promises to give us all the help we need from

His Holy Spirit as we leave our old lives behind and embrace the new life He graciously offers (Romans 8: 9-14[21]).

Jesus desires to turn our lives around for our benefit and His glory!

CHAPTER 2
Scripture Verses

1. **Ephesians 4:20-24:** But that isn't what you learned about Christr. [21] Since you have heard about Jesus and have learned the truth that comes from him, [22] throw off your old sinful nature and your former way of life, which is corrupted by lust and deception. [23] Instead, let the Spirit renew your thoughts and attitudes. [24] Put on your new nature, created to be like God—truly righteous and holy.

2. **James 2:19:** You say you have faith, for you believe that there is one God. Good for you! Even the demons believe this, and they tremble in terror.

3. **2 Corinthians 7:10:** For the kind of sorrow God wants us to experience leads us away from sin and results in salvation. There's no regret for that kind of sorrow. But worldly sorrow, which lacks repentance, results in spiritual death.

4. **Galatians 5:16-17:** So I say, let the Holy Spirit guide your lives. Then you won't be doing what your sinful nature craves. [17] The sinful nature wants to do evil, which is just the opposite of what the Spirit wants. And the Spirit gives us desires that are the opposite of what the sinful nature desires. These two forces are constantly fighting each other, so you are not free to carry out your good intentions.

5. **Galatians 5:19-21:** When you follow the desires of your sinful nature, the results are very clear: sexual immorality, impurity, lustful pleasures, [20] idolatry, sorcery, hostility, quarreling, jealousy, outbursts of anger, selfish ambition, dissension, division, [21] envy, drunkenness, wild parties, and other sins like these. Let me tell you again, as I have before, that anyone living that sort of life will not inherit the Kingdom of God.

6. **1 Corinthians 13:4-7:** Love is patient and kind. Love is not jealous or boastful or proud [5] or rude. It does not demand its own way. It is not irritable, and it keeps no record of being wronged. [6] It does not rejoice about injustice but rejoices whenever the truth wins

out. [7] Love never gives up, never loses faith, is always hopeful, and endures through every circumstance.

7. **Galatians 5:22-24:** But the Holy Spirit produces this kind of fruit in our lives: love, joy, peace, patience, kindness, goodness, faithfulness, [23] gentleness, and self-control. There is no law against these things! [24] Those who belong to Christ Jesus have nailed the passions and desires of their sinful nature to his cross and crucified them there.

8. **Deuteronomy 4:29:** But from there you will search again for the Lord your God. And if you search for him with all your heart and soul, you will find him.

9. **Isaiah 57:15:** The high and lofty one who lives in eternity, the Holy One, says this: "I live in the high and holy place with those whose spirits are contrite and humble. I restore the crushed spirit of the humble and revive the courage of those with repentant hearts."

10. **Matthew 4:17:** From then on Jesus began to preach, "Repent of your sins and turn to God, for the Kingdom of Heaven is near."

11. **Acts 2:38:** Peter replied, "Each of you must repent of your sins and turn to God, and be baptized in the name of Jesus Christ for the forgiveness of your sins. Then you will receive the gift of the Holy Spirit."

12. **Acts 20:21:** I have had one message for Jews and Greeks alike - the necessity of repenting from sin and turning to God, and of having faith in our Lord Jesus.

13. **1 John 1:9-10:** [9] But if we confess our sins to him, he is faithful and just to forgive us our sins and to cleanse us from all wickedness. [10] If we claim we have not sinned, we are calling God a liar and showing that his word has no place in our hearts.

14. **Matthew 6:33:** Seek the Kingdom of God above all else, and live righteously, and he will give you everything you need.

15. **2 Samuel 22:20:** He led me to a place of safety; he rescued me because he delights in me.

16. **Psalm 18:19:** He led me to a place of safety; he rescued me because he delights in me.

17. **Psalm 37:23:** The Lord directs the steps of the godly. He delights in every detail of their lives.

18. **Isaiah 62:4:** Never again will you be called "The Forsaken City" or "The Desolate Land." Your new name will be "The City of God's Delight" and "The Bride of God," for the Lord delights in you and will claim you as his bride.

19. **Deuteronomy 14:2:** You have been set apart as holy to the Lord your God, and he has chosen you from all the nations of the earth to be his own special treasure.

20. **Deuteronomy 26:18:** The Lord has declared today that you are his people, his own special treasure, just as he promised, and that you must obey all his commands.

21. **Romans 8:9-14:** But you are not controlled by your sinful nature. You are controlled by the Spirit if you have the Spirit of God living in you. (And remember that those who do not have the Spirit of Christ living in them do not belong to him at all.) [10] And Christ lives within you, so even though your body will die because of sin, the Spirit gives you life because you have been made right with God. [11] The Spirit of God, who raised Jesus from the dead, lives in you. And just as God raised Christ Jesus from the dead, he will give life to your mortal bodies by this same Spirit living within you. [12] Therefore, dear brothers and sisters you have no obligation to do what your sinful nature urges you to do. [13] For if you live by its dictates, you will die. But if through the power of the Spirit you put to death the deeds of your sinful nature, you will live. [14] For all who are led by the Spirit of God are children of God.

CHAPTER THREE
FAITH

The word *faith* is described as 'reliance, loyalty, and complete trust'. Faith can be used in many contexts, such as a simple belief that your car will get you to your destination. Or, you may have a more complex faith, such as a steadfast trust in God, Whom you cannot see.

We find one of the best biblical definitions of faith in the book of Hebrews. It says: "Faith is the confident assurance that what we hope for is going to happen. It is the evidence of things we cannot yet see" (Hebrews 11:1[1]). As we believe and obey Jesus through faith, we are given hope for the future, because we gain understanding as to why we are here on earth, and where we are going to be after death.

God gave us His written Word, the Bible, because He *wants* us to know Him. His desire is for us to learn how to live our lives according to His principles. Biblical faith is displayed by our trust that God will love us, direct us, protect us, and empower us, no matter what our circumstances. This is the type of faith that God wants every Christian to experience.

We read in Hebrews 11:6 "And it is impossible to please God without faith. Anyone who wants to come to him must believe that God exists and that he rewards those who sincerely seek him". Our faith literally determines the kind of relationship we will have with the Lord. Most of us realize after we come to the Lord that our 'spiritual eyes' were closed before we BELIEVED (1 Corinthians 2:13-16[2]). We were unable to understand the principles that Jesus spoke of, because they seemed so contrary to our human wisdom.

Faith is the reason we believe that Jesus is alive and working in our lives. Those who do not have Jesus, and therefore, the Spirit of God, living inside of them cannot understand why we place ourselves in God's hands, and why we live our lives according to His ways and His plans.

Coming to faith is not a one-time decision. Although it begins with our choice to accept Jesus into our hearts, it continues to *grow* through a dynamic process. As we consistently decide to choose the Lord's ways over our own, we will begin to experience the 'abundant life' He promises. This abundance includes peace, joy, hope, and purpose in our lives. And as we *continue* to remain in close relationship with Him, He shows us His faithfulness through every trial. Ultimately, we realize that He will remain true to His Word no matter what happens in our lives. This is active faith.

Where Does My Faith Come From?

Now let's examine where our faith comes from. We read in Romans 12:3[3] that our faith originates from God, not ourselves. So we see that it is not our job to *obtain* our faith; it is our job to *receive* it. The Bible also says that faith comes from Jesus, who is also God (2 Peter 1:1[4]). And there are times that God will give an *extra measure* of faith to some people. This type of faith is a supernatural gift of the Holy Spirit, called a "Spiritual Gift" (1 Corinthians 12:9[5]).

Romans 10:17[6] says that faith also comes from hearing the Word of God. So our faith will continue to be refined and strengthened as we read the Bible and listen to biblical teaching. However, we need to obey what we have learned from God in order to have our faith increased and matured. It's pretty amazing that our faith comes from God, Jesus, the Holy Spirit, and the Bible!

Practical Faith

Some important questions people ask are "How should my faith be demonstrated as I conduct myself in this world? What does it mean to live as a person of faith? And what's the point of having faith except to get to heaven?" James 2:14-26[7] talks about 'faith in action'. *People with genuine, active faith in Jesus exhibit a likeness to Him.* And they go about doing good works because that is the *fruit* – the byproduct - of their relationship with Him (James 3:13[8]).

Another question people have about their faith is if their prayers really make a difference. Maybe you wonder if God is hearing your prayers at all. We can get frustrated when what we have been praying for never comes to pass. We may start to question our faith. The answer lies in the character of God. He alone possesses the power to see into the future, and as such, He knows what is best for us.

Even though we think we have the best answer to our problems and we pray in that direction, the truth is, our solutions may not fit into the plans God has for us in that particular situation. And it's possible that our plans aren't be the best option for us or others. I know there have been many times I was glad that God didn't answer my prayers the way I thought He should! We are to pray about everything, but leave the outcome to Him.

You Just Don't Have Enough Faith!

Maybe you're a Christian and you've been told "You just don't have enough faith and that's why your prayers are not being answered". This is unbiblical! There are many reasons why our prayers are not answered the way we have asked. Our faith originates from God so all who genuinely believe in Him have plenty of faith.

One reason our prayers may not be answered is that we're asking for things that are not in our best interest (James 4:1-3[9]). Or, we may have hidden sin in our lives that needs to be confessed and repented of before our prayers are heard (James 5:16-17[10]).

Maybe we find ourselves praying for salvation for another person. It is definitely God's will that they be saved! However, if they refuse to accept Jesus into their lives, it may have little to do with *our* faith and prayers, and more to do with *their* stubborn rebellion. God will not force Himself on us. In this way, our prayers may go unanswered (Hebrews 10:39[11]).

We must be in intimate relationship with the Lord if we are to have His heart and mind. As we become more like Him through this union, our prayers will begin to change so they are more in alignment with His will. When the desires of our hearts are changed, we won't care as much about the fancy cars, huge houses, and bigger bank accounts.

Our new focus will be on other people – those who are less fortunate than ourselves. We will begin to ask for strength to help the lost and needy. God will empower us to share our faith so others can know the Lord. It is only then that God will be able to abundantly bless our prayers, because we will be asking according to HIS will.

Faith, Not Works

There are plenty of religions where people have to do different kinds of service or rituals to please God. Sometimes, they have to bear many children so they will be 'represented' in heaven. Or, they are required to knock on their quota of doors. Or they must bring in enough converts to their faith in order to have done enough 'good works' to please God and earn His favor. It is heartbreaking to see people wonder if they are doing *enough to* please God, and living in fear for their salvation every day.

However, the God of the Bible is fully delighted with those who trust in faith that *Jesus already paid their sin debt.* Our bill is paid up in full! Jesus knew we would have never been able to "earn enough" to pay for our transgressions in our own power, so He lovingly did it for us.

In fact, the Bible says "People are counted as righteous **not** because of their works, but because of their *faith*" (Romans 4:5[12]). While good works are a *result* of our relationship with Jesus, these "works" spring from our love for Him, not because of our fear that we're not doing enough to earn our way.

About That Fruit

We have learned that genuine faith is *faith that produces fruit* (Matthew 7:17[13]; Luke 6:45[14]). The Bible uses the word *fruit* to describe the visible results of our work for God, just as a tree produces fruit that we can see. Part of this fruit includes sharing Jesus frequently with others as the Holy Spirit leads. It means bringing glory to God every day, in whatever you do (1 Corinthians 10:31[15]). It also includes ministering to the Body of Christ - The Church. This kind of fruit is *eternal* - it will last forever.

Those who are attached to the Vine (Who is JESUS), bear much fruit, which brings glory to the Father (John 15:5-8[16]). Jesus says that every tree that does not produce good fruit will be chopped down and thrown in the fire (Matthew 3:10[17])! God wants the fruit that is produced in our lives to bring Him praise and honor, and He wants to use us to bring the lost into relationship with Him (Matthew 25:20-45[18]).

We receive salvation so we can be close to God and go to heaven forever, but we are also to use the time, talent, and money we have been given to further His Kingdom. God's primary concern is for people, and He uses those who deeply and faithfully love His Son to reach this unsaved world on His behalf.

Decide by faith to believe in and trust Jesus!

CHAPTER 3
Scripture Verses

1.   **Hebrews 11:1:** Faith shows the reality of what we hope for; it is the evidence of things we cannot see.

2.   **1 Corinthians 2:13-16:** When we tell you these things, we do not use words that come from human wisdom. Instead, we speak words given to us by the Spirit, using the Spirit's words to explain spiritual truths. [14] But people who aren't spiritual can't receive these truths from God's Spirit. It all sounds foolish to them and they can't understand it, for only those who are spiritual can understand what the Spirit means. [15] Those who are spiritual can evaluate all things, but they themselves cannot be evaluated by others. [16] For, "Who can know the Lord's thoughts? Who knows enough to teach him?" But we understand these things, for we have the mind of Christ.

3.   **Romans 12:3:** Because of the privilege and authority God has given me, I give each of you this warning: Don't think you are better than you really are. Be honest in your evaluation of yourselves, measuring yourselves by the faith God has given us.

4.   **2 Peter 1:1:** This letter is from Simon Peter, a slave and apostle of Jesus Christ. I am writing to you who share the same precious faith we have. This faith was given to you because of the justice and fairness of Jesus Christ, our God and Savior.

5.   **1 Corinthians 12:9:** The same Spirit gives great faith to another, and to someone else the one Spirit gives the gift of healing.

6.   **Romans 10:17:** So faith comes from hearing, that is, hearing the Good News about Christ.

7.   **James 2:14-26:** What good is it, dear brothers and sisters, if you say you have faith but don't show it by your actions? Can that kind of faith save anyone? [15] Suppose you see a brother or sister who has no food or clothing, [16] and you say, "Good-bye and have a good day; stay warm and eat well"—but then you don't give that person

any food or clothing. What good does that do? [17] So you see, faith by itself isn't enough. Unless it produces good deeds, it is dead and useless. [18] Now someone may argue, "Some people have faith; others have good deeds." But I say, "How can you show me your faith if you don't have good deeds? I will show you my faith by my good deeds." [19] You say you have faith, for you believe that there is one God. Good for you! Even the demons believe this, and they tremble in terror. [20] How foolish! Can't you see that faith without good deeds is useless? [21] Don't you remember that our ancestor Abraham was shown to be right with God by his actions when he offered his son Isaac on the altar? [22] You see, his faith and his actions worked together. His actions made his faith complete. [23] And so it happened just as the Scriptures say: "Abraham believed God, and God counted him as righteous because of his faith." He was even called the friend of God. [24] So you see, we are shown to be right with God by what we do, not by faith alone. [25] Rahab the prostitute is another example. She was shown to be right with God by her actions when she hid those messengers and sent them safely away by a different road. [26] Just as the body is dead without breath, so also faith is dead without good works.

8. **James 3:13:** If you are wise and understand God's ways, prove it by living an honorable life, doing good works with the humility that comes from wisdom.

9. **James 4:1-3:** What is causing the quarrels and fights among you? Don't they come from the evil desires at war within you? [2] You want what you don't have, so you scheme and kill to get it. You are jealous of what others have, but you can't get it, so you fight and wage war to take it away from them. Yet you don't have what you want because you don't ask God for it. [3] And even when you ask, you don't get it because your motives are all wrong—you want only what will give you pleasure.

10. **James 5:16-17:** Confess your sins to each other and pray for each other so that you may be healed. The earnest prayer of a righteous person has great power and produces wonderful results. [17] Elijah

was as human as we are, and yet when he prayed earnestly that no rain would fall, none fell for three and a half years!

11. **Hebrews 10:39:** But we are not like those who turn away from God to their own destruction. We are the faithful ones, whose souls will be saved.

12. **Romans 4:5:** But people are counted as righteous, not because of their work, but because of their faith in God who forgives sinners.

13. **Matthew 7:17:** A good tree produces good fruit, and a bad tree produces bad fruit.

14. **Luke 6:45:** A good person produces good things from the treasury of a good heart, and an evil person produces evil things from the treasury of an evil heart. What you say flows from what is in your heart.

15. **1 Corinthians 10:31:** So whether you eat or drink, or whatever you do, do it all for the glory of God.

16. **John 15:5-8:** (Jesus said) "Yes, I am the vine; you are the branches. Those who remain in me, and I in them, will produce much fruit. For apart from me you can do nothing. [6] Anyone who does not remain in me is thrown away like a useless branch and withers. Such branches are gathered into a pile to be burned. [7] But if you remain in me and my words remain in you, you may ask for anything you want, and it will be granted! [8] When you produce much fruit, you are my true disciples. This brings great glory to my Father."

17. **Matthew 3:10:** Even now the ax of God's judgment is poised, ready to sever the roots of the trees. Yes, every tree that does not produce good fruit will be chopped down and thrown into the fire.

18. **Matthew 25:20-45:** The servant to whom he had entrusted the five bags of silver came forward with five more and said, 'Master, you gave me five bags of silver to invest, and I have earned five more.' [21] "The master was full of praise. 'Well done, my good and faithful servant. You have been faithful in handling this small amount, so now I will give you many more responsibilities. Let's celebrate

together!' [22] "The servant who had received the two bags of silver came forward and said, 'Master, you gave me two bags of silver to invest, and I have earned two more.' [23] "The master said, 'Well done, my good and faithful servant. You have been faithful in handling this small amount, so now I will give you many more responsibilities. Let's celebrate together!' [24] "Then the servant with the one bag of silver came and said, 'Master, I knew you were a harsh man, harvesting crops you didn't plant and gathering crops you didn't cultivate. [25] I was afraid I would lose your money, so I hid it in the earth. Look, here is your money back.' [26] "But the master replied, 'You wicked and lazy servant! If you knew I harvested crops I didn't plant and gathered crops I didn't cultivate, [27] why didn't you deposit my money in the bank? At least I could have gotten some interest on it.' [28] "Then he ordered, 'Take the money from this servant, and give it to the one with the ten bags of silver. [29] To those who use well what they are given, even more will be given, and they will have an abundance. But from those who do nothing, even what little they have will be taken away. [30] Now throw this useless servant into outer darkness, where there will be weeping and gnashing of teeth.' [31] "But when the Son of Man comes in his glory, and all the angels with him, then he will sit upon his glorious throne. [32] All the nation will be gathered in his presence, and he will separate the people as a shepherd separates the sheep from the goats. [33] He will place the sheep at his right hand and the goats at his left. [34] "Then the King will say to those on his right, 'Come, you who are blessed by my Father, inherit the Kingdom prepared for you from the creation of the world. [35] For I was hungry, and you fed me. I was thirsty, and you gave me a drink. I was a stranger, and you invited me into your home. [36] I was naked, and you gave me clothing. I was sick, and you cared for me. I was in prison, and you visited me.' [37] "Then these righteous ones will reply, 'Lord, when did we ever see you hungry and feed you? Or thirsty and give you something to drink? [38] Or a stranger and show you hospitality? Or naked and give you clothing? [39] When did we ever see you sick or in prison and visit you?' [40] "And the King will say, 'I tell you the truth, when you did it to one of the least of these my brothers and sisters, you were doing it to me!' [41] "Then the King will turn to those on the left and say, 'Away with you, you cursed ones, into the eternal fire prepared for the devil and his demons [42] For I was hungry, and you didn't feed me. I was thirsty, and you didn't give me a drink. [43] I was a stranger, and you didn't invite me into your home. I was naked, and you didn't give me clothing. I was sick and in prison, and you didn't visit me.' [44] "Then they will reply, 'Lord, when did we ever see you hungry or thirsty or a stranger or naked or sick or in prison, and not help you?' [45] "And he will answer, 'I tell you the truth, when you refused to help the least of these my brothers and sisters, you were refusing to help me.'

SALVATION

What comes to your mind when you hear the phrase "You need to be saved?"

Maybe you think of "born again Christians" – sort of like the "love child" of the 60's – the kind of people who are *unusually* happy and carefree, but not really "living in reality". Others believe their life is just fine, and they can save themselves, thank you very much. And some are so terrified of being vulnerable that they trust no one, and won't even consider being "saved" from anything. But let's find out what the Bible teaches about this essential component to Christianity.

<u>Salvation Is Love Confirmed</u>

We learned from our first chapter on *Sin* that we are lost and unable to save ourselves. Whether we like to admit it or not, we all have a desperate need to be saved *from* our sin. Part of the problem is, we *like* our sin. We detest it when others try to tell us we aren't living the way we should.

We prefer to think we have the "freedom" to do whatever we want, but "liberty" without self-discipline is actually enslavement (1 Peter 2:16[1]; 2 Peter 2:19[2]). How many times have you "gotten what you wanted", but it turned out to be much less meaningful than you had imagined before you acquired it? Most often, we will find that a great void is created when we live only to please ourselves. The truth is, we only achieve genuine freedom as we surrender to the Lord Jesus Christ (Galatians 3:22[3]). But we cannot do this in our own power. Thus, we see our need for salvation.

The word *salvation* means "to save". God is perfect, holy, and pure. Therefore, He *must* punish sin! Since we are separated from God by our sin, and the debt we owe for our sin is too great for us to pay, we need a savior – someone who will rescue us by paying our debt to bring us back to God (Matthew 9:12-13[4]; John 3:16-17[5]). Jesus came to earth – as God in the flesh – for that very purpose. Indeed, Jesus' very name means "Savior or Salvation" (Matthew 1:21[6]).

As God Himself lovingly interceded on our behalf, He took upon Himself the punishment *we deserved* for our sin (Ephesians 1:3-8[7]; Galatians 3:13[8]; 1 John 2:2[9]). Jesus paid our price – which was death - so He could restore a relationship with us (2 Corinthians 5:17-21[10]; 1Peter 2:24[11]). This is called *reconciliation.* When we realize our need for God and come to Him in repentance, we are given new life and are born into the family of God. This act of "paying our debt" is called *redemption.*

Why Would God Pay Our Debt?

It's incredibly difficult to understand why God loves us enough to have died for us. Especially when we are so undeserving. However, it is HIS desire that we be saved (1Timothy 2:3-4[12]). His love for us is deep and vast – and we are unable to comprehend it. However, He has made a way for us to accept that our sin is paid for, so we can come into His presence without guilt and shame. His Spirit continues to work in us, making *us* righteous – virtuous, honorable, and upright - so that we will be able to commune with Him in His holiness.

Jesus tells us in His own words "I came to seek and save the lost" (Luke 19:9-10[13]). The "lost" are those who are living apart from a close relationship with the true, living God. HE took the initiative to help you out of your sin. HE wants to erase the stain of your sin and your guilt so He can have an intimate bond with you (Psalm 51:1-2[14]). Sin and guilt need to be dealt with, because these are the very obstacles that keep us from seeking and enjoying God.

Why Did Jesus Have to Die for Me?

As we have already learned, God has a fury against sin. We see examples of this anger in the Old Testament. The story of the Flood in Noah's time, as well as Sodom and Gomorrah, were two examples of God's judgment of sin. We know there are both biblical and historical stories of entire cities and cultures that were wiped out because of immorality. We have even seen the downhill spiral in our own country, because we have accepted sin as normal. Good is now called evil, and evil, good (Isaiah 5:20[15]).

Jesus was chosen to pay for our sin, because only *God Himself* could have handled His own wrath. He knows that human beings are completely unable to withstand His overwhelming judgment; we would be destroyed by it. That's why *Jesus* took our penalty. As God, He was the only one who was able to handle the weight of His own hatred towards sin.

And that's exactly what the Gospel is - it's the Good News that Jesus died in my place and now I can experience a close relationship with God. In effect, He traded my wickedness for His righteousness – which is His own right standing with God (Titus 3:4-7[16]).

None of us are good enough to be in relationship with God (Romans 3:21-26[17]). Nevertheless, He adores us no matter what we have done. Although there is a responsibility on our part to stay in fellowship with Him and obey His ways, He did the work we were completely unable to do ourselves. And now, as authentic Christians, we now have perfect status with the Father (Colossians 1:21-22[18]).

All Paths Do NOT Lead To God

There are many religions in the world, and you have probably heard the saying "All paths lead to God". But Jesus said that HE is the only way to the Father (John 14:6[19]; 17:3[20]; Acts 4:11-12[21]). People who have not accepted Jesus into their hearts cannot understand this truth. Many people claim to be *spiritual*, but if they haven't received salvation from Jesus Christ, they literally have the wrong "spirit" working in them. People who don't have God's Spirit think that Jesus' claim is narrow-minded, rigid, and foolish (1 Corinthians 2:14[22]).

However, if you think about it, all religions *except* Christianity lack the beauty of **God** *reaching down to help* **us**. All other "faiths" are based on *man's* ability to master his own destiny. There may be requirements to "appease the gods", which demand great work and human effort. Other religions promote the idea of putting ourselves on the "throne" of our lives, so we can make all of life's decisions without any help from God. But both of these methods leave us with the same problem – our sin nature is still in full effect. Only God can truly change the human heart.

Jesus Himself tells us that we need to be "born again" in order to see into the supernatural dimension of His Kingdom (John 3:1-8[23]). Once we place our faith in Jesus, His Holy Spirit gives us a new understanding of spiritual things. For example, we begin to comprehend the Bible on a new level, because the Holy Spirit is the only one who can reveal Scripture to us.

We start to experience new feelings and ways of relating. Upon salvation, our spirits literally become 'alive' through supernatural transformation. As a result, we gain a new awareness of God. And as we progress in our Christian faith, we will come to love the Savior on a deeper level and desire to please Him with more of our lives.

Jesus sacrificed His own life so that we could be free to live in loving obedience to Him. We have always had the "liberty" to sin, but now, with the Holy Spirit's power, we can exhibit the character of Jesus in our lives (Colossians 3:12-15[24]). This includes putting others first, and demonstrating His very character, which is love, joy, peace, patience, kindness, goodness, gentleness, faithfulness, and self-control. The Bible tells us we are saved so that we can now do the work that God has called us to (Ephesians 2:8-10[25]).

Loving and obeying Jesus will change every part of your life

CHAPTER 4
Scripture Verses

1. **1 Peter 2:16:** For you are free, yet you are God's slaves, so don't use your freedom as an excuse to do evil.

2. **2 Peter 2:19:** They promise freedom, but they themselves are slaves of sin and corruption. For you are a slave to whatever controls you.

3. **Galatians 3:22:** But the Scriptures declare that we are all prisoners of sin, so we receive God's promise of freedom only by believing in Jesus Christ.

4. **Matthew 9:12-13:** [12] When Jesus heard this, he said, "Healthy people don't need a doctor—sick people do." [13] Then he added, "Now go and learn the meaning of this Scripture: 'I want you to show mercy, not offer sacrifices.' For I have come to call not those who think they are righteous, but those who know they are sinners."

5. **John 3:16-17:** [16] "For this is how God loved the world: He gave his one and only Son, so that everyone who believes in him will not perish but have eternal life. [17] God sent his Son into the world not to judge the world, but to save the world through him."

6. **Matthew 1:21:** And she will have a son, and you are to name him Jesus, for he will save his people from their sins.

7. **Ephesians 1:3-8:** [3] All praise to God, the Father of our Lord Jesus Christ, who has blessed us with every spiritual blessing in the heavenly realms because we are united with Christ. [4] Even before he made the world, God loved us and chose us in Christ to be holy and without fault in his eyes. [5] God decided in advance to adopt us into his own family by bringing us to himself through Jesus Christ. This is what he wanted to do, and it gave him great pleasure. [6] So we praise God for the glorious grace he has poured out on us who belong to his dear Son. [7] He is so rich in kindness and grace that he purchased our freedom with the blood of his Son and forgave our

sins. [8] He has showered his kindness on us, along with all wisdom and understanding.

8. **Galatians 3:13:** But Christ has rescued us from the curse pronounced by the law. When he was hung on the cross, he took upon himself the curse for our wrongdoing. For it is written in the Scriptures, "Cursed is everyone who is hung on a tree."

9. **1 John 2:2:** He himself is the sacrifice that atones for our sins - and not only our sins but the sins of all the world.

10. **2 Corinthians 5:17-21:** [17] This means that anyone who belongs to Christ has become a new person. The old life is gone; a new life has begun! [18] And all of this is a gift from God, who brought us back to himself through Christ. And God has given us this task of reconciling people to him. [19] For God was in Christ, reconciling the world to himself, no longer counting people's sins against them. And he gave us this wonderful message of reconciliation. [20] So we are Christ's ambassadors; God is making his appeal through us. We speak for Christ when we plead, "Come back to God!" [21] For God made Christ, who never sinned, to be the offering for our sin, so that we could be made right with God through Christ.

11. **1 Peter 2:24:** He personally carried our sins in his body on the cross so that we can be dead to sin and live for what is right. By his wounds you are healed.

12. **1 Timothy 2:3-4:** This is good and pleases God our Savior, [4] who wants everyone to be saved and to understand the truth.

13. **Luke 19:9-10:** [9] Jesus responded, "Salvation has come to this home today, for this man has shown himself to be a true son of Abraham. [10] For the Son of Man came to seek and save those who are lost."

14. **Psalm 51:1-2:** [1] Have mercy on me, O God, because of your unfailing love. Because of your great compassion, blot out the stain of my sins. [2] Wash me clean from my guilt. Purify me from my sin.

15. **Isaiah 5:20:** What sorrow for those who say that evil is good and good is evil, that dark is light and light is dark, that bitter is sweet and sweet is bitter.

16. **Titus 3:4-7:** [4] But when God our Savior revealed his kindness and love, [5] he saved us, not because of the righteous things we had done, but because of his mercy. He washed away our sins, giving us a new birth and new life through the Holy Spirit. [6] He generously poured out the Spirit upon us through Jesus Christ our Savior. [7] Because of his grace he made us right in his sight and gave us confidence that we will inherit eternal life.

17. **Romans 3:21-26:** [21] But now God has shown us a way to be made right with him without keeping the requirements of the law, as was promised in the writings of Moses and the prophets long ago. [22] We are made right with God by placing our faith in Jesus Christ. And this is true for everyone who believes, no matter who we are. [23] For everyone has sinned; we all fall short of God's glorious standard. [24] Yet God, in his grace, freely makes us right in his sight. He did this through Christ Jesus when he freed us from the penalty for our sins. [25] For God presented Jesus as the sacrifice for sin. People are made right with God when they believe that Jesus sacrificed his life, shedding his blood. This sacrifice shows that God was being fair when he held back and did not punish those who sinned in times past, [26] for he was looking ahead and including them in what he would do in this present time. God did this to demonstrate his righteousness, for he himself is fair and just, and he makes sinners right in his sight when they believe in Jesus.

18. **Colossians 1:21-22:** [21] This includes you who were once far away from God. You were his enemies, separated from him by your evil thoughts and actions. [22] Yet now he has reconciled you to himself through the death of Christ in his physical body. As a result, he has brought you into his own presence, and you are holy and blameless as you stand before him without a single fault.

19. **John 14:6:** Jesus told him, "I am the way, the truth, and the life. No one can come to the Father except through me."

20. **John 17:3:** And this is the way to have eternal life - to know you, the only true God, and Jesus Christ, the one you sent to earth.

21. **Acts 4:11-12:** [11] For Jesus is the one referred to in the Scriptures, where it says, 'The stone that you builders rejected has now become the cornerstone.' [12] There is salvation in no one else! God has given no other name under heaven by which we must be saved."

22. **1 Corinthians 2:14:** But people who aren't spiritual can't receive these truths from God's Spirit. It all sounds foolish to them and they can't understand it, for only those who are spiritual can understand what the Spirit means.

23. **John 3:1-8:** There was a man named Nicodemus, a Jewish religious leader who was a Pharisee. [2] After dark one evening, he came to speak with Jesus. "Rabbi," he said, "we all know that God has sent you to teach us. Your miraculous signs are evidence that God is with you." [3] Jesus replied, "I tell you the truth, unless you are born again, you cannot see the Kingdom of God." [4] "What do you mean?" exclaimed Nicodemus. "How can an old man go back into his mother's womb and be born again?" [5] Jesus replied, "I assure you, no one can enter the Kingdom of God without being born of water and the Spirit. [6] Humans can reproduce only human life, but the Holy Spirit gives birth to spiritual life. 7 So don't be surprised when I say, 'You must be born again.' [8] The wind blows wherever it wants. Just as you can hear the wind but can't tell where it comes from or where it is going, so you can't explain how people are born of the Spirit."

24. **Colossians 3:12-15:** [12] Since God chose you to be the holy people he loves, you must clothe yourselves with tenderhearted mercy, kindness, humility, gentleness, and patience. [13] Make allowance for each other's faults, and forgive anyone who offends you. Remember, the Lord forgave you, so you must forgive others. [14] Above all, clothe yourselves with love, which binds us all together in perfect harmony. [15] And let the peace that comes from Christ rule in your hearts. For

as members of one body you are called to live in peace. And always be thankful.

25. **Ephesians 2:8-10:** [8] God saved you by his grace when you believed. And you can't take credit for this; it is a gift from God. [9] Salvation is not a reward for the good things we have done, so none of us can boast about it. [10] For we are God's masterpiece. He has created us anew in Christ Jesus, so we can do the good things he planned for us long ago.

CHAPTER FIVE
WHAT IS THE BIBLE?

The Holy Bible is the only book on earth that is completely and literally inspired by God Himself. Indeed, the Greek word for *inspired* means "divinely breathed in", and as such, the Bible is called "The Word of God". And it is one of the primary methods by which God reveals Himself to mankind.

There are 66 books in the Bible with approximately 33 authors, written over a period of nearly 1,500 years. Some people argue that the Bible was merely written by man, and is therefore untrustworthy. But Scripture is clear that the Holy Spirit used these men to write exactly what *God* wanted written (1 Thessalonians 2:13[1]; 2 Peter 1:20-21[2]).

God is free of error – Perfect, Holy, and True. Therefore, His words to us are absolute truth. We tread on very dangerous ground when we take the Bible "cafeteria style" – choosing what we will and will not believe about it. Just because someone rejects its truth doesn't mean they won't be accountable to it before God.

Since GOD uses the Bible to explain *Himself* to us, we must accept it as His complete, authoritative, and divine revelation. Even if we don't *like* subjects like hell, judgment, or personal responsibility, it is essential that we accept, believe, and act on what *God* has told us about these critical issues.

It's All About *Jesus*
Amazingly, we read that Jesus Christ is the major thread that runs through the Bible from the beginning to the end. This is just one proof of the Bible's

divine nature, because it is humanly impossible for all of these writers to have written about a common theme – especially when they didn't even know each other or communicate amongst themselves. Furthermore, the majority of Scripture was written centuries before Jesus even walked the earth.

The first two thirds of God's Word is the Old Testament (OT). Soon after God created mankind, He chose the nation of Israel, whom He called the Israelites, or Jews, to proclaim His love and glory to the world (Deuteronomy 7:6[3]). He made an eternal covenant - which is an agreement or promise between two parties – with them. In this covenant, God essentially told them that if they devoted their entire lives to Him, He would be their God and they would be His beloved people (Leviticus 26:12[4]; Deuteronomy 6:4-9[5])." The entire OT is based around this relationship.

Unfortunately, the Israelites had an "on again, off again" relationship with God for hundreds of years. They vacillated between loving and serving God, to turning away from Him and worshiping idols. We read many stories where God punished them severely, but this was not because He hated them; rather, it was because He loved them and wanted them to see that turning from Him would never bring them love, peace, joy, and life. We find the same problem among his followers today. That's why taking God and His Word very seriously is so important. He wants us to be completely devoted to Him.

Interestingly, the Jews are still one of the most hated people in the world. Satan hates them, and subsequently, many people who do not follow after God hate them. This is partly because they are the beloved of God, and partly because Jesus came from this Jewish bloodline. It is miraculous that their country is only a third as big as the state of Florida, and yet they have won war after war, and have kept their tiny little country intact. God has truly preserved them.

The New Testament

The last third of the Bible is called the New Testament (NT), which is a New Covenant between God and those who believe in, love, and serve Jesus (2 Corinthians 3:6[6]; Hebrews 10:16[7]). These people are called Christians. Christians make up the Church, which is an embodiment of this new covenant relationship. Now, whether you are male or female, black or white, rich or poor, Jew or non-Jew, you are part of God's chosen family – *if* you genuinely place your faith in Christ and seek to live according to His will.

As we enter into this relationship, it is imperative to cultivate a healthy fear of God. This "fear" is not being terrified – rather, it is a respect and awe that we must possess in order to truly worship and obey the Lord. God is a majestic God, and He *deserves* the glory, honor, and adoration of human beings. Indeed, man will not be able to ignore, reject, and scorn the Living God forever.

The Power Of The Bible

We read that the Bible is **alive** (Hebrews 4:12[8]). It is a supernatural book, able to uncover and deal with the root of sin in the human heart. Because God is Truth and He cannot lie, His Word to us is the only source of real Truth in the universe. Incredibly, the Bible, just like the Father, Son, and Spirit, is eternal in nature (Mark 13:31[9]; 1 Peter 1:25[10]).

In order to understand the Scriptures, we need the Holy Spirit to reveal its meaning to us. Those who do not have the Spirit living in them cannot comprehend its content (1 Corinthians 2:10-16[11]). That's why people who don't believe in Jesus find the Word of God to be boring and irrelevant. The Spirit is the one who brings the Word to life for us and allows it to mold and shape our thinking, our wills, and our hearts (Psalm 19:7-9[12]).

We desperately need an eternal, rock-solid truth to base our lives on, because the world system we live in is full of lies, manipulation, hatred and greed. Haven't we all been let down by the government? By science? By medicine? By friends, family, bosses – people in general? That's because this world is built on human wisdom. Man's inborn nature is deceitful and wicked (Jeremiah 17:9[13])! Indeed, even when we seek God's methods, we are still prone to error because of our human frame.

So How Can We Live According to God's Principles?

There is an answer to our dilemma and it is found in the Bible! Scripture is able to cleanse our consciences and purify our motives (Jeremiah 23:29[14]; Ephesians 5:25-26[15]; 1Timothy 1:5[16]). As we read the Word regularly and obey it wholeheartedly, it is able to make us holy (John 17:17[17]). The Spirit of God and the Bible are able to impart genuine life to us (John 6:63[18]; 1 Peter 1:23[19]). It teaches us right from wrong and is able to correct our thinking (2 Timothy 3:16-17[20]). It changes the way we think so that we can understand and follow God's will for our lives (Romans 12:2[21]).

The Bible is called the Sword of the Spirit, because through the power of the Holy Spirit, it is able to cut through the lies we believe and destroy our old way of reasoning (Ephesians 6:17[22]). It's incredible that Jesus, just as the Bible, is also called The Word of God (John 1:1[23]; Revelation 19:13[24]) and The Word of Life (1 John 1:1[25]). As God, His very words ARE the Bible! He is the Living Word and the Bible is the Written Word.

The Scriptures are a lamp to our feet and a light to our path in life (Psalm 119:105[26]). It illuminates dangers in our Christian walk and keeps us safe, *if* we obey it. It is able to keep us from lying to ourselves (Psalm 119:29[27]). It has the power to save our souls as we read it and follow its directives (James 1:21[28]). It can keep us from sinning (Psalm 119:11[29]), and keep us pure (Psalm 119:9[30]). It also has the power to save us from the evil one, Satan (1 John 2:14[31]) *as we let it* live and dwell in our hearts.

Remember, we receive salvation through faith in Christ, but we need to keep being cleansed to *remain* in Him, which is what the Bible does for us. The Scriptures remind us that we need to obey the Word, or else we are just fooling ourselves (James 1:22-25[32]; 1 Peter 2:8[33]). Indeed, we literally show our love for Jesus by obeying His Word (John 14:15[34], John 14:21[35]; 1 John 2:5[36]). And we will be blessed by following our Lord's commands (Revelation 1:3[37]; 22:7[38]). God surely has a tight grip on us, so we don't have to constantly worry about "falling away". But our relationship with Him will certainly be tainted if we don't make an effort to stay close to Jesus!

This is not an exhaustive list on how wonderful and powerful the Bible is. But it gives us an overview of how essential it is to study it and do what it says. I cannot stress enough how important it is to make Bible reading a daily part of your life. And don't just "read" it – study it! Pray throughout your reading. Ask questions such as "How does this relate to my life?" Or "God, what are You trying to say to me?" Look up the maps and see where your text is taking place. You can search the references to other similar passages that are located on the inside margin of your Bible. Write your thoughts and prayers down. It's a great experience and you will get to know God so much better. Please, consider getting up a little earlier every morning if necessary.

Start each day with the Book of Life! If you're a night owl, read your Bible nightly. The truth is, you will *never* have the quality of life you desire with God if you fail to meet with Him regularly in His Word. If you're a new Christian, the book of John is a great place to start, because it highlights who Jesus is.

Studying the Bible is fun! It will make your life in Christ so much deeper, and infinitely more alive. It is a lifeline to God, and a Rock to keep you stable in this ever-changing and often dangerous world (Isaiah 26:3-4[39]). The Word imparts God's heart to us, reveals His purpose for us, and shows His loving direction for us. You will never regret spending time getting to know God through the Bible. He is worthy of the time and effort you put forth as you seek to know Him.

Your life will literally be transformed as you study God's Word!

CHAPTER 5
Scripture Verses

1. **1 Thessalonians 2:13:** Therefore, we never stop thanking God that when you received his message from us, you didn't think of our words as mere human ideas. You accepted what we said as the very word of God—which, of course, it is. And this word continues to work in you who believe.

2. **2 Peter 1:20-21:** [20] Above all, you must realize that no prophecy in Scripture ever came from the prophet's own understanding, [21] or from human initiative. No, those prophets were moved by the Holy Spirit, and they spoke from God.

3. **Deuteronomy 7:6:** For you are a holy people, who belong to the Lord your God. Of all the people on earth, the Lord your God has chosen you to be his own special treasure.

4. **Leviticus 26:12**: I will walk among you; I will be your God, and you will be my people.

5. **Deuteronomy 6:4-9:** [4] "Listen, O Israel! The Lord is our God, the Lord alone. [5] And you must love the Lord your God with all your heart, all your soul, and all your strength. [6] And you must commit yourselves wholeheartedly to these commands that I am giving you today. [7] Repeat them again and again to your children. Talk about them when you are at home and when you are on the road, when you are going to bed and when you are getting up. [8] Tie them to your hands and wear them on your forehead as reminders. [9] Write them on the doorposts of your house and on your gates."

6. **2 Corinthians 3:6:** He has enabled us to be ministers of his new covenant. This is a covenant not of written laws, but of the Spirit. The old written covenant ends in death; but under the new covenant, the Spirit gives life.

7. **Hebrews 10:16:** "This is the new covenant I will make with my people on that day, say the Lord: I will put my laws in their hearts, and I will write them on their minds."

8. **Hebrews 4:12:** For the word of God is alive and powerful. It is sharper than the sharpest two-edged sword, cutting between soul and spirit, between joint and marrow. It exposes our innermost thoughts and desires.

9. **Mark 13:31:** Heaven and earth will disappear, but my words will never disappear.

10. **1 Peter 1:25:** But the word of the Lord remains forever. And that word is the Good News that was preached to you.

11. **1 Corinthians 2:10-16:** [10] But it was to us that God revealed these things by his Spirit. For his Spirit searches out everything and shows us God's deep secrets. [11] No one can know a person's thoughts except that person's own spirit, and no one can know God's thoughts except God's own Spirit. [12] And we have received God's Spirit (not the world's spirit), so we can know the wonderful things God has freely given us. When we tell you these things, we do not use words that come from human wisdom. Instead, we speak words given to us by the Spirit, using the Spirit's words to explain spiritual truths. [14] But people who aren't spiritual can't receive these truths from God's Spirit. It all sounds foolish to them and they can't understand it, for only those who are spiritual can understand what the Spirit means. [15] Those who are spiritual can evaluate all things, but they themselves cannot be evaluated by others. [16] For, "Who can know the Lord's thoughts? Who knows enough to teach him?" But we understand these things, for we have the mind of Christ.

12. **Psalm 19:7-9:** The instructions of the Lord are perfect, reviving the soul. The decrees of the Lord are trustworthy, making wise the simple. [8] The commandments of the Lord are right, bringing joy to the heart. The commands of the Lord are clear, giving insight for living. [9] Reverence for the Lord is pure, lasting forever. The laws of the Lord are true; each one is fair.

13. **Jeremiah 17:9:** "The human heart is the most deceitful of all things, and desperately wicked. Who really knows how bad it is?"

14. **Jeremiah 23:29:** "Does not my word burn like fire?" says the Lord. "Is it not like a mighty hammer that smashes a rock to pieces?"

15. **Ephesians 5:25-26:** ²⁵ For husbands, this means love your wives, just as Christ loved the church. He gave up his life for her ²⁶ to make her holy and clean, washed by the cleansing of God's word.

16. **1 Timothy 1:5:** The purpose of my instruction is that all believers would be filled with love that comes from a pure heart, a clear conscience, and genuine faith.

17. **John 17:17:** Make them holy by your truth; teach them your word, which is truth.

18. **John 6:63:** The Spirit alone gives eternal life. Human effort accomplishes nothing. And the very words I have spoken to you are spirit and life.

19. **1 Peter 1:23:** For you have been born again, but not to a life that will quickly end. Your new life will last forever because it comes from the eternal, living word of God.

20. **2 Timothy 3:16-17:** ¹⁶ All Scripture is inspired by God and is useful to teach us what is true and to make us realize what is wrong in our lives. It corrects us when we are wrong and teaches us to do what is right. ¹⁷ God uses it to prepare and equip his people to do every good work.

21. **Romans 12:2:** Don't copy the behavior and customs of this world, but let God transform you into a new person by changing the way you think. Then you will learn to know God's will for you, which is good and pleasing and perfect.

22. **Ephesians 6:17:** Put on salvation as your helmet, and take the sword of the Spirit, which is the word of God.

23. **John 1:1:** In the beginning the Word already existed. The Word was with God, and the Word was God.

24. **Revelation 19:13:** He wore a robe dipped in blood, and his title was the Word of God.

25. **1 John 1:1:** We proclaim to you the one who existed from the beginning, whom we have heard and seen. We saw him with our own eyes and touched him with our own hands. He is the Word of life.

26. **Psalm 119:105:** Your word is a lamp to guide my feet and a light for my path.

27. **Psalm 119:29:** Keep me from lying to myself; give me the privilege of knowing your instructions.

28. **James 1:21:** So get rid of all the filth and evil in your lives, and humbly accept the word God has planted in your hearts, for it has the power to save your souls.

29. **Psalm 119:11:** I have hidden your word in my heart, that I might not sin against you.

30. **Psalm 119:9:** How can a young person stay pure? By obeying your word.

31. **1 John 2:14:** I have written to you who are God's children because you know the Father. I have written to you who are mature in the faith because you know Christ, who existed from the beginning. I have written to you who are young in the faith because you are strong. God's word lives in your hearts, and you have won your battle with the evil one.

32. **James 1:22-25:** [22] But don't just listen to God's word. You must do what it says. Otherwise, you are only fooling yourselves. [23] For if you listen to the word and don't obey, it is like glancing at your face in a mirror. [24] You see yourself, walk away, and forget what you look like. [25] But if you look carefully into the perfect law that sets you free, and if you do what it says and don't forget what you heard, then God will bless you for doing it.

33. **1 Peter 2:8:** And, "He is the stone that makes people stumble, the rock that makes them fall." They stumble because they do not obey God's word, and so they meet the fate that was planned for them.

34. **John 14:15:** [15] "If you love me, obey my commandments."

35. **John 14:21:** [21] "Those who accept my commandments and obey them are the ones who love me. And because they love me, my Father will love them. And I will love them and reveal myself to each of them."

36. **1 John 2:5:** But those who obey God's word truly show how completely they love him. That is how we know we are living in him.

37. **Revelation 1:3:** God blesses the one who reads the words of this prophecy to the church, and he blesses all who listen to its message and obey what it says, for the time is near.

38. **Revelation 22:7:** "Look, I am coming soon! Blessed are those who obey the words of prophecy written in this book."

39. **Isaiah 26:3-4:** [3] You will keep in perfect peace all who trust in you, all whose thoughts are fixed on you! [4] Trust in the Lord always, for the Lord God is the eternal Rock.

WHO IS GOD?

In this chapter, we will learn about God, the Father - the first Person of the Triune Godhead. *Triune* means "three in unity". Jesus is the Second Person, and the Holy Spirit is the Third Person in this marvelous Union. They are all distinct Persons, and are equal in power and majesty. They were all present at Creation, and they sustain the universe together. We call this Godhead the *Trinity*. It is a difficult concept to grasp, but so is electricity. And we all believe that electricity exists ☺

God the Father possesses many facets to His personality. For example, just as a man might be called a husband, a father, an employee, and a son, God's names reflect His different roles. He is called *Lord,* which means "Master" or "Owner". In Hebrew, He is also called *Jehovah Jireh,* which means "God will Provide". He is also named *El Shaddai,* which means "God Almighty". Another of His names is *Adonai,* which stands for "The Lord Supreme".

In The Beginning
The very beginning of the Bible records that God is the Creator of the universe (Genesis 1:1[1]; Psalm 24:1-2[2]). He is also the Creator of the human race (Genesis 2:4-7[3]; Psalm 139:13-16[4]). We may "nod" our assent to this statement, implying "Of course God created everything"! But because we have often been taught in school that we are the result of a "big bang" event, or we come from apes and only the strongest of us survive, we tend to have a mixture of beliefs about the conflicting things we have heard and learned over the years about God's creation.

However, believing any other truth than we were created uniquely by the hand of God can lead us to many psychological and spiritual ills later in life. Every theory *except* Creation disregards the beauty of God reaching into time to personally fashion humankind.

One of the most damaging mindsets we can have is to lose sight of how precious each one of us is to God. Our very life is extremely important, because God Himself intricately formed us, and He intimately breathed life into us (Job 10:8a[5]; 33:4[6]).

Human Versus Divine

In the first chapter of this book, we learned that our human hearts are deceitful and wicked. We need someone outside of ourselves – more powerful and capable and moral than us- to change our sinful condition. While it is true that a person may live a relatively "decent" life apart from God, the reality is that without Him in our lives, we are incapable of having a pure heart with right motives. More importantly, if we are not in a relationship with God through Jesus Christ, it will be impossible for us to get to Heaven (John 14:6).

God is altogether different than we are. Although we are created *in His image,* sin has marred our ability to accurately reflect His glory to this world. For instance, He *hates* the evil we do (Proverbs 6:16-19[8]). We tend to love our sin, our idols, and our selfish ways. However, God will not tolerate sin, even though He loves all people. The main reason He detests sin is *love* – because He knows that our sin separates us from Him.

God loves justice and He is always fair. People often want to blame Him for the horrible atrocities in the world, but a great portion of the devastation we see is a direct result of man's greed, hatred, and lust, as well as their refusal to submit to and obey God. When God created mankind, He intended for us to live in a perfect world – the one we now long for. However, sin has introduced death, decay, and destruction into our lives. And let's not forget that the enemy of our souls, Satan, directly adds to the evil we see.

The Character Of God

Human "character" is a sum of traits, learned behavior, and natural, inborn affinities that a person possesses. Our character largely determines our choices, because who we *are* = what we *do*. No matter what we "say" - we end up "doing" what we really feel like doing. Often, we do as we please without regard to others.

God, on the other hand, has an "absolute" character. He has always been the same and will be the same forever. He doesn't change because of feelings, location, circumstances, or outside influences. He always acts in perfect love and perfect justice. That is His "character" – that's who He IS. His personality traits and qualities are the theme of this chapter.

The Bible tells us that when the Spirit of God indwells us after we receive Jesus into our lives, much of *our* character is supernaturally changed (Romans 12:2[9]). Having a relationship with the Almighty Creator *should* radically change you! We literally become new creations at salvation (2 Corinthians 5:17[10]). We are given new hearts, minds, and desires (Ezekiel 36:26-27[11]; Hebrews 8:10[12]).

This Scripture in Hebrews is referring to the Jews. Remember, they were God's chosen people in the Old Testament. Jews and Gentiles (non-Jews) were considered two separate groups, because the Jewish people were set apart by God from the rest of the world. He chose them to display His glory and His ways to others. And they were the only ethnic group who believed in the One True God, as opposed to the rampant idol worship that was so common amongst other cultures.

But since the New Testament, Jews and Gentiles have now been brought together. This came about because Jesus went to the Cross for *all* people so they would have the ability to *choose* to be set free from their sins. Now, if we are born again – regardless of our heritage –we are "God's people" and are set apart to display His glory to the world.

Incidentally, even though I am a Gentile and have the amazing privilege of being God's child, I believe He will always hold a very special place in His heart for the Jewish people.

As we study this lesson, try to visualize how lovely, beautiful, true, faithful and good our God really is. And also remember just how majestic, fierce, righteous, and holy He is! Then commit your whole being to Him, and determine to let Him change you to be more like Himself.

***

God the Father is Spirit (John 4:24[13]). He is not mortal (Job 9:32[14]), which means that He is not human, and was not created. This eternal state is called *pre-existent*. It's difficult for us to understand, but God has always been alive. He lived before time began and He will live forever, which is described as *immortal*. This is where our desire to live for eternity originates (Ecclesiastes 3:11[15]). What is so amazing is that Jesus is also Pre-Existent and Immortal (John 1:1[16]), as He Himself is also God – God in the flesh.

God is a jealous God (Exodus 20:5a[17]). However, this jealousy is not like human jealousy; this is the kind of 'jealousy' a nurturing husband has for his beloved wife – born out of a healthy love to ensure her protection. He is guarding the union he has with her so that the world does not infringe upon them. God uses this analogy often by calling His people "His Bride". Just like a caring and supporting husband, He is also called our refuge and our strength (Psalm 46:1[18]). There is only One true God (2 Samuel 7:22[19]). The word *sovereign* in this Scripture means "In absolute control; Supreme; Self-Governing". He alone is the ruler of the universe (Isaiah 43:10[20]; 44: 6-8[21]). He is a supernatural God and works in miraculous and astounding ways (Psalm 77:14[22]). *Nothing* is too great or difficult for God to perform. And while He does overthrow man's foolish plans at times, the only thing He will not overpower is our human choice if we refuse to love and obey Him. Genuine love always allows the freedom to choose.

God is called our Rock, because He is completely stable in all of His ways (Psalm 18:1-3[23]; Psalm18:30-33[24]). He is a Shield and a Defender of those who love, trust, and obey Him. He is the Only True Savior, and as such, He is the only one to offer us authentic salvation (Isaiah 45:21-22[25]).

He Is A Personal God

When we pray to God, He hears and answers our prayers. In fact, the Bible says "He bends down to hear us" (Psalm 116:2[26]). Of course, He is spirit and doesn't literally bend down, but it is a word picture for us so we can imagine just how tender and attentive our God really is.

And as we pray, we need to be aware that the outcome of our prayers will often be answered in ways completely different than what we had asked. Although we should pray for everything, we should expect God's answers to be in complete accordance with His will (1 John 5:14[27]). Even Jesus was subject to intense suffering, so we should expect no less at times in our own lives (Matthew 26:39[28]).

A wise person knows that God always responds to our prayers in the most beneficial way. In His wisdom, He alone knows that we may need hardship or suffering to bring us closer to Him, or to remove impurities in our lives. And don't be surprised when your prayers are answered in remarkable ways, because He is a mighty, exciting, powerful and eternal God (Deuteronomy 10:21[29])!

God IS love (1 John 4:8[30]). He doesn't just "love us" – His *base nature* is love, so He cannot *help* but love us. But this isn't our type of love – emotionally charged, conditional, and ever-changing. God's love is constant and He always has our best interest at heart. This unique kind of love is called *agape love* and is outlined in 1 Corinthians 13: 4-6-7[31].

You may have heard this Scripture before, but ask yourself how regularly you exhibit even one of these traits. I know that personally, I have a hard time consistently showing just one of these demonstrations of love! This is the type of love that God wants us to have for Him and for others, but it is humanly impossible without His Spirit working in us.

Another of God's characteristics is Justice. This is the part of God that we may not understand, or even like. But because He is a Holy God, He must be fair. Just as we wouldn't expect a good parent to be so "loving" that they never said 'no' or dispensed discipline, God loves us unconditionally - but He must also punish disobedience. That is why we see disastrous consequences in the Bible for those who do not obey Him (Psalm 31:23[32]; 145:20[33]).

The Bible says that God is the only One in the universe who is all-knowing, which is called *omniscient.* Therefore, He alone can deliver us from sin and danger. God is everywhere – a term called *omnipresent* so He sees everything at all times, all at once.

However, He is not "*in* everything" as some religions claim. He, through His Holy Spirit, only comes to live inside those who have allowed Jesus Christ to redeem their lives. He only inhabits the hearts of those who love Him. Additionally, God is all-powerful, which is called *omnipotent*, so He is truly able to do whatever He chooses.

This is comforting for believers, because we know that He is in charge of the world, even when it looks like it's spinning out of control (Psalm 22:28[34]). Our great hope is the certainty that God will one day reign in complete truth and goodness for eternity. But for now, Satan is the god of this world, and we will experience evil until he is destroyed.

God Is Magnificent

God's ways and thoughts are much different than ours (Isaiah 55:8-9[35]). This is important to understand, because we often want to "fit Him into our box", when we really need to "fit ourselves into HIS box". People want to live life on their own terms – and often just "tack" God onto their lives.

For example, there are people who call themselves "Christians" just so they can feel good about being "right with God". But they have not truly surrendered their will and lives to Him. This is a very dangerous position to live in. He is adamant that you are either for Him or against Him. God makes it clear in His Word: We are to love Him, serve Him, and obey Him with our entire being (Deuteronomy 7:9[36], 12[37]; 10:12-13[38]; 11:1[39], 22[40]).

God deserves our adoration! He is gracious, compassionate, and merciful. He loves to forgive us when we are genuinely sorrowful and we are ready to turn from our sin (Psalm 25:4-15[41]; 116:5[42]; Jonah 4:2b[43]). He will always love us no matter what we have done. However, we cannot claim to be in fellowship with Him if we do not seek His will above our own and determine to live according to His standards (1 John 1:6[44]). Mistakes will be made, for sure, but our overall lifestyle should reflect our relationship with Him.

It gives God great pleasure to bring you into His family! He is passionate about guiding, teaching, and empowering you (Ephesians 1:5[45])! If you do not know how to submit your life to God, ask Him and He will show you.

He promises to give you the power to obey Him (Philippians 2:13[46]). You can learn what He wants from you and what He offers you by reading the Bible, talking to Him in prayer, and being involved in a Christ-centered church.

God desires to have an intimate relationship with you!

CHAPTER 6
Scripture Verses

1. **Genesis 1:1:** In the beginning God created the heavens and the earth.

2. **Psalm 24:1-2:** [1] The earth is the Lord's, and everything in it. The world and all its people belong to him. [2] For he laid the earth's foundation on the seas and built it on the ocean depths.

3. **Genesis 2:4-7:** [4] This is the account of the creation of the heavens and the earth. When the Lord God made the earth and the heavens, [5] neither wild plants nor grains were growing on the earth. For the Lord God had not yet sent rain to water the earth, and there were no people to cultivate the soil. [6] Instead, springs came up from the ground and watered all the land. [7] Then the Lord God formed the man from the dust of the ground. He breathed the breath of life into the man's nostrils, and the man became a living person.

4. **Psalm 139:13-16:** [13] You made all the delicate, inner parts of my body and knit me together in my mother's womb. [14] Thank you for making me so wonderfully complex! Your workmanship is marvelous; how well I know it. [15] You watched me as I was being formed in utter seclusion, as I was woven together in the dark of the womb. [16] You saw me before I was born. Every day of my life was recorded in your book. Every moment was laid out before a single day had passed.

5. **Job 10:8a:** You formed me with your hands; you made me...

6. **Job 33:4:** For the Spirit of God has made me, and the breath of the Almighty gives me life.

7. **John 14:6:** Jesus told him, "I am the way, the truth, and the life. No one can come to the Father except through me."

8. **Proverbs 6:16-19:** [16] There are six things the Lord hates - no, seven things he detests: [17] haughty eyes, a lying tongue, hands that kill the

innocent,[18] a heart that plots evil, feet that race to do wrong,[19] a false witness who pours out lies, a person who sows discord in a family.

9. **Romans 12:2:** Don't copy the behavior and customs of this world, but let God transform you into a new person by changing the way you think. Then you will learn to know God's will for you, which is good and pleasing and perfect.

10. **2 Corinthians 5:17:** This means that anyone who belongs to Christ has become a new person. The old life is gone; a new life has begun!

11. **Ezekiel 36:26-27:** [26] And I will give you a new heart, and I will put a new spirit in you. I will take out your stony, stubborn heart and give you a tender, responsive heart. [27] And I will put my Spirit in you so that you will follow my decrees and be careful to obey my regulations.

12. **Hebrews 8:10:** But this is the new covenant I will make with the people of Israel on that day, says the Lord: I will put my laws in their minds, and I will write them on their hearts. I will be their God, and they will be my people.

13. **John 4:24:** For God is Spirit, so those who worship him must worship in spirit and in truth.

14. **Job 9:32:** God is not a mortal like me, so I cannot argue with him or take him to trial.

15. **Ecclesiastes 3:11:** Yet God has made everything beautiful for its own time. He has planted eternity in the human heart, but even so, people cannot see the whole scope of God's work from beginning to end.

16. **John 1:1:** In the beginning the Word already existed. The Word was with God, and the Word was God.

17. **Exodus 20:5a:** "You must not bow down to them or worship them, for I, the Lord your God, am a jealous God who will not tolerate your affection for any other gods..."

18. **Psalm 46:1:** God is our refuge and strength, always ready to help in times of trouble.

19. **2 Samuel 7:22:** "How great you are, O Sovereign Lord! There is no one like you. We have never even heard of another God like you!"

20. **Isaiah 43:10:** "But you are my witnesses, O Israel!" says the Lord. "You are my servant. You have been chosen to know me, believe in me, and understand that I alone am God. There is no other God - there never has been, and there never will be."

21. **Isaiah 44: 6-8:** This is what the Lord says - Israel's King and Redeemer, the Lord of Heaven's Armies: "I am the First and the Last; there is no other God. [7] Who is like me? Let him step forward and prove to you his power. Let him do as I have done since ancient times when I established a people and explained its future. [8] Do not tremble; do not be afraid. Did I not proclaim my purposes for you long ago? You are my witnesses—is there any other God? No! There is no other Rock - not one!"

22. **Psalm 77:14:** You are the God of great wonders! You demonstrate your awesome power among the nations.

23. **Psalm 18:1-3:** [1] I love you, Lord; you are my strength. [2] The Lord is my rock, my fortress, and my savior; my God is my rock, in whom I find protection. He is my shield, the power that saves me, and my place of safety. [3] I called on the Lord, who is worthy of praise, and he saved me from my enemies.

24. **Psalm18:30-33:** [30] God's way is perfect. All the Lord's promises prove true. He is a shield for all who look to him for protection. [31] For who is God except the Lord? Who but our God is a solid rock? [32] God arms me with strength, and he makes my way perfect. [33] He makes me as surefooted as a deer, enabling me to stand on mountain heights.

25. **Isaiah 45:21-22:** [21] Consult together, argue your case. Get together and decide what to say. Who made these things known so long ago? What idol ever told you they would happen? Was it not I, the Lord? For there is no other God but me, a righteous God and Savior. There is none but me. [22] Let all the world look to me for salvation! For I am God; there is no other.

26. **Psalm 116:1-2:** [1] I love the Lord because he hears my voice and my prayer for mercy. [2] Because he bends down to listen, I will pray as long as I have breath!

27. **1 John 5:14:** And we are confident that he hears us whenever we ask for anything that pleases him.

28. **Matthew 26:39:** He went on a little farther and bowed with his face to the ground, praying, "My Father! If it is possible, let this cup of suffering be taken away from me. Yet I want your will to be done, not mine."

29. **Deuteronomy 10:21:** He alone is your God, the only one who is worthy of your praise, the one who has done these mighty miracles that you have seen with your own eyes.

30. **1 John 4:8:** But anyone who does not love does not know God, for God is love.

31. **1 Corinthians 13: 4-6-7:** [4] Love is patient and kind. Love is not jealous or boastful or proud [5] or rude. It does not demand its own way. It is not irritable, and it keeps no record of being wronged. [6] It does not rejoice about injustice but rejoices whenever the truth wins out. [7] Love never gives up, never loses faith, is always hopeful, and endures through every circumstance.

32. **Psalm 31:23:** Love the Lord, all you godly ones! For the Lord protects those who are loyal to him, but he harshly punishes the arrogant.

33. **Psalm 145:20:** The Lord protects all those who love him, but he destroys the wicked.

34. **Psalm 22:28:** For royal power belongs to the Lord. He rules all the nations.

35. **Isaiah 55:8-9:** [8] "My thoughts are nothing like your thoughts," says the Lord. "And my ways are far beyond anything you could imagine. [9] For just as the heavens are higher than the earth, so my ways are higher than your ways and my thoughts higher than your thoughts."

36. **Deuteronomy 7:9:** Understand, therefore, that the Lord your God is indeed God. He is the faithful God who keeps his covenant for a

thousand generations and lavishes his unfailing love on those who love him and obey his commands.

37. **Deuteronomy 7:12:** If you listen to these regulations and faithfully obey them, the Lord your God will keep his covenant of unfailing love with you, as he promised with an oath to your ancestors.

38. **Deuteronomy 10:12-13:** [12] "And now, Israel, what does the Lord your God require of you? He requires only that you fear the Lord your God, and live in a way that pleases him, and love him and serve him with all your heart and soul. [13] And you must always obey the Lord's commands and decrees that I am giving you today for your own good."

39. **Deuteronomy 11:1:** You must love the Lord your God and always obey his require ments, decrees, regulations, and commands.

40. **Deuteronomy 11:22:** Be careful to obey all these commands I am giving you. Show love to the Lord your God by walking in his ways and holding tightly to him.

41. **Psalm 25:4-15:** [4] Show me the right path, O Lord; point out the road for me to follow. [5] Lead me by your truth and teach me, for you are the God who saves me. All day long I put my hope in you. [6] Remember, O Lord, your compassion and unfailing love, which you have shown from long ages past. [7] Do not remember the rebellious sins of my youth. Remember me in the light of your unfailing love, for you are merciful, O Lord. [8] The Lord is good and does what is right; he shows the proper path to those who go astray. [9] He leads the humble in doing right, teaching them his way. [10] The Lord leads with unfailing love and faithfulness all who keep his covenant and obey his demands. [11] For the honor of your name, O Lord, forgive my many, many sins. [12] Who are those who fear the Lord? He will show them the path they should choose. [13] They will live in prosperity, and their children will inherit the land. [14] The Lord is a friend to those who fear him. He teaches them his covenant. [15] My eyes are always on the Lord, for he rescues me from the traps of my enemies.

42. **Psalm 116:5:** How kind the Lord is! How good he is! So merciful, this God of ours!

43. **Jonah 4:2b:** I knew that you are a merciful and compassionate God, slow to get angry and filled with unfailing love. You are eager to turn back from destroying people.

44. **1 John 1:6:** So we are lying if we say we have fellowship with God but go on living in spiritual darkness; we are not practicing the truth.

45. **Ephesians 1:5:** God decided in advance to adopt us into his own family by bringing us to himself through Jesus Christ. This is what he wanted to do, and it gave him **great pleasure**.

46. **Philippians 2:13:** For God is working in you, giving you the desire and the power to do what pleases him.

WHO IS JESUS?

The name *Jesus* literally means "Savior". *Jesus* is His Greek name, but it is of Hebrew origin, derived from the name *Yehoshua,* or *Joshua,* meaning "Jehovah saves". Jesus came from heaven, became human, and lived among mankind. His purpose was to bring people back into relationship with God, because they had been separated from Him by sin (John 3:16-17[1]).

Another Hebrew root word for *Jesus* is *Yasha,* meaning "to save, to free, to defend, to deliver, to preserve, or to get victory". Salvation is the free gift that we need to choose to receive from God in order to be saved from our sins. It is available to everyone in the world. However, Jesus is a personal Savior, and this means that a relationship needs to be established with Him through our conscious choice. Only those who trust in Him and love Him will be delivered from sin and hell, and given eternal life. Those who have entered into this union with Jesus find that He truly saves us, frees us, defends us, delivers us, preserves us, and gives us victory!

Jesus is also named *Christ,* which means "Chosen One" or "Anointed One". This is the equivalent of the Hebrew name *Messiah.* Jesus is also called *Lord.* The capitalized name *Lord* in the Old Testament is also translated "Jehovah," which is God's name. It means Eternal or Self-Existent, signifying that He was not created.

When Jesus is called *Lord* in the New Testament, the word is "kurios" which means Supreme God, Master, or Sir. Names are extremely important in the Bible, so for God and Jesus to be called the same name is very significant. These shared names are clear indicators that Jesus and God have equal status – they are both God.

This brings a very important point to light. In the Jewish culture and religion, Jehovah (Father) God was so holy - so far removed from mankind because of His great power and authority - that the Jews were afraid to even speak to Him directly (Exodus 20:18-19[2]). In fact, they later developed a tradition in which they didn't even *say* His name. They spelled Jehovah "JHWH" because they felt it was disrespectful to use His full name. This is not commanded in Scripture, but it goes to show how awestruck they felt about God.

Additionally, the Israelites believed that the words ascribed to God - *especially* His names - were not to be used for *any other person, purpose, or thing* except for God. For example, when He is referred to as "Almighty God", the Jews refrained from calling anything else 'almighty'. So....to ascribe JESUS with the same names as Almighty God was *blasphemy* in their minds. Blasphemy is a biblical term that means "to verbally defame or to despise" (God). To slander or hate God was unthinkable, and it was worthy of capital punishment – **death** (Leviticus 24:13-16[3])!

Jesus Is God

The Holy Bible teaches us that Jesus IS God - in the flesh (John 1:1[4]). In this Scripture, Jesus is called "The Word", which was understood to mean "The Agent of Creation". *The Word* also was described as "The Architect of Creation". Of course, only *God* can create and sustain life. This truth about Jesus is repeated in 1 John 1:1[5], where He is also called "The Word of Life". In fact, Jesus Himself tells us that He is able to give eternal life, and that the Father and He are One (John 10:28-30[6]).

This is the fundamental (essential or basic) truth that separates ALL religions from Christianity. Most religions around the world believe that Jesus was a "good man" or a "prophet", but if you question them carefully, you will find they deny Jesus as Creator and the Gateway to Eternal Life.

There are even faiths that "claim" to be Christians, but the bottom line is this: Do they believe in the Deity - the Godhood - of Jesus Christ? This truth needs to be dealt with before one becomes a true Christian, because it is the absolute and foundational truth that genuine Christianity is based upon (John 1:18[7]).

Remember in our previous studies on "Sin" and "Repentance", that only *God* could have handled His own anger against sin. A human without a Divine nature would have been destroyed. When Jesus went to the Cross, He was enduring *all of God's wrath for the sins of the world!*

Additionally, in the Old Testament, God required a perfect lamb or bull for the blood sacrifice for people's sins. Therefore, Jesus, as *our* blood sacrifice, was obligated to be perfect. So if He had sin in His life, He would have been disqualified - He would have been too imperfect to be the Sacrifice to pay for our sin. Therefore, *God Himself* – the only Perfect One who was Jesus -came in the flesh to destroy the sin-barrier that separated man from Himself (2 Corinthians 5:21[8]). It cannot be overstated how essential it is to believe in Jesus' divine *and* human nature.

The Bible tells us that God revealed *everything He was doing* to Jesus (John 5:20-23[9]). Mere man would not be able to handle that kind of information! We read again in this passage that Jesus is able to give life (vs 21), which only *God* has the power to do. Jesus is also given all authority to judge, and only *God* is supreme enough to judge man (vs 22). Additionally, we read that Jesus will be given the same honor as the Father (vs 23), which makes them equal in majesty.

To continue, another name for Jesus is *Emmanuel*, meaning "*God* with us". The Jews would *never* give anyone this kind of honor except for God Himself. The religious leaders were furious because Jesus quite clearly equated Himself with God the Father (Mark 14:60-65[10]). They wanted Him crucified for blasphemy (John 10:31-33[11])!

Think about it – if He was just a lunatic, they would have ignored Him. But they were terrified of His power and authority! In fact, the very phrase He uses to describe Himself in the passage we just read - I AM – attests to His Godhood status.

When Jesus says "I AM", He is referring back to the Old Testament. God directed Moses to tell the Israelites that I AM sent you (i.e. GOD HIMSELF sent you) (Exodus 3:12-15[12]). This Scripture also says "Tell them Yahweh has sent you". *Yahweh* is translated "The Lord", or "Jehovah". Jesus applied this very passage to HIMSELF! Moreover, Jesus even had the audacity to say that He existed before Abraham, *who lived 2,000 years before Jesus was even born* (John 8:58-59[13])!

Jesus persistently used this "I AM" phrase to describe Himself: I AM the Bread of Life (John 6:35[14]). I AM the Light of the World (John 8:12[15]). I AM the Gate (John 10:7-9[16]). I AM the Good Shepherd (John 10:11[17]). I AM the True Grapevine (John 15:1[18]). The words I AM, used in these contexts, are not just our regular words for *"I am* hungry". Translated from the Hebrew and the Greek, these words are full of divine power - so dynamic that they literally caused men fall to the ground (John 18:4-6[19])!

Amazingly, there were over 300 prophecies about Jesus in the Old Testament (for example, Isaiah 9:6[20]; 11:1-5[21]; Isaiah 53[22]; Micah 5:2-4[23]). You can see these prophecies for yourself at: accordingtothescriptures. org/prophecy/353prophecies.html.

Don't forget that these Scriptures were written anywhere from 400 to 2,000 years before Jesus even came to the earth in the flesh! And since most of these prophecies have already come to pass with 100% accuracy (some of them are still to be fulfilled in the future), we know that we can trust the Bible as the solid Truth of God.

Jesus Is Worthy

The Bible tells us that "In Jesus, the **fullness of God** dwells in human form (Colossians 2:9-10[24]). Think about that. God, in all of His power and splendor, lived IN Jesus! If Jesus were not Divine, He would have been incapable of that kind of weight and responsibility. This Scripture also says that as God, He is far above all rulers and authorities (vs 10).

Jesus is the Living God and Savior (1Timothy 4:10[25]; 2 Pet 1:1[26]). It is interesting that both God the Father and Jesus are referred to as Savior (Isaiah 43:11[27]; Titus 2:13-14[28]). They are both named "The Rock" (1 Samuel 2:2[29]; 1 Peter 2:5-8[30]). This verse in1 Peter is actually referring back to Isaiah 8:14[31], when it's talking about God the Father. But Paul refers to *the Old Testament Rock as Christ* in 1 Corinthians 10:3-4[32]!

We see the beauty and magnificence of Jesus Christ as the Supreme God in Colossians 1:15-20[33]. Jesus is the King of kings and Lord of lords (1Timothy 6:15[34]). In fact, God the Father literally refers to His Son Jesus *as God* (Hebrews 1:6-12[35]). The Bible tells us that "Jesus is always the same and will live forever", asserting that He is Eternal and was not a created being; He came directly from heaven (1 Corinthians 15:47[36]).

Jesus is forever our Great High Priest (Hebrews 7:24-28[37]).The High Priest in the Old Testament was a mediator – the "go-between" from man to God. Jesus IS that person now. Again, one of the deep truths and mysteries of the Gospel is that Jesus is fully man, but He is also fully God. As God, He possesses power and authority over the universe; as a human, He is able to "plead our case" before God (Romans 8:34[38]).

The previous passage in Hebrews 7 also tells us that Jesus is holy and blameless, unstained by sin. Only *God* is *that* pure! God the Father chose Jesus long before the earth was even created to be our sacrifice, so that we could receive eternal life (1 Peter 1:18-20[39]). He is our Sinless Redeemer, our Healer, and the Guardian of our souls (1 Peter 2:22-25[40]; 1 John 3:5[41]). In His perfect Majesty, every knee on earth will eventually bow to Him. It is our choice as to whether we will bend our knee to Him in fear or in love (Philippians 2:6-11[42]).

While Jesus is our Loving Savior, the Gentle Lamb and the Suffering Servant, He is at the same time, the Almighty Judge (2 Corinthians 5:10[43]), and ruler over everything. He is worthy of *eternal* praise - and only God is worthy of this fervent and everlasting praise (Romans 9:5b[44]). Jesus is also the first to rise from the dead with a glorified spiritual body (Revelation 1:5[45]).

He is far above every leader or power, and all things are under His authority (Ephesians 1:21[46]).He is the commander of all the rulers of the world, and He will overpower evil once and for all at the end of time (Revelation 19:11-16[47]). No other person, religion, or ideology in this world can compare to Him!

This is why Jesus is the *only way* to heaven (John 14:6-9b[48]).

Praise the High and Powerful Name of Jesus!!

CHAPTER 7
Scripture Verses

1. **John 3:16-17:** [16] "For this is how God loved the world: He gave his one and only Son, so that everyone who believes in him will not perish but have eternal life. [17] God sent his Son into the world not to judge the world, but to save the world through him."

2. **Exodus 20:18-19:** [18] When the people heard the thunder and the loud blast of the ram's horn, and when they saw the flashes of lightning and the smoke billowing from the mountain, they stood at a distance, trembling with fear. [19] And they said to Moses, "You speak to us, and we will listen. But don't let God speak directly to us, or we will die!"

3. **Leviticus 24:13-16:** [13] Then the Lord said to Moses, [14] "Take the blasphemer outside the camp, and tell all those who heard the curse to lay their hands on his head. Then let the entire community stone him to death. [15] Say to the people of Israel: Those who curse their God will be punished for their sin. [16] Anyone who blasphemes the Name of the Lord must be stoned to death by the whole community of Israel. Any native-born Israelite or foreigner among you who blasphemes the Name of the Lord must be put to death."

4. **John 1:1:** In the beginning the Word already existed. The Word was with God, and the Word was God.

5. **1 John 1:1:** We proclaim to you the one who existed from the beginning, whom we have heard and seen. We saw him with our own eyes and touched him with our own hands. He is the Word of life.

6. **John 10:28-30:** [28] "I give them eternal life, and they will never perish. No one can snatch them away from me, [29] for my Father has given them to me, and he is more powerful than anyone else. No one can snatch them from the Father's hand. [30] The Father and I are one."

7. **John 1:18:** No one has ever seen God. But the unique One (Jesus), who is himself God, is near to the Father's heart. He has revealed God to us.

8. **2 Corinthians 5:21:** For God made Christ, who never sinned, to be the offering for our sin, so that we could be made right with God through Christ.

9. **John 5:20-23:** [20] For the Father loves the Son and shows him everything he is doing. In fact, the Father will show him how to do even greater works than healing this man. Then you will truly be astonished. [21] For just as the Father gives life to those he raises from the dead, so the Son gives life to anyone he wants. [22] In addition, the Father judges no one. Instead, he has given the Son absolute authority to judge, [23] so that everyone will honor the Son, just as they honor the Father. Anyone who does not honor the Son is certainly not honoring the Father who sent him.

10. **Mark 14:60-65:** [60] Then the high priest stood up before the others and asked Jesus, "Well, aren't you going to answer these charges? What do you have to say for yourself?" [61] But Jesus was silent and made no reply. Then the high priest asked him, "Are you the Messiah, the Son of the Blessed One?" [62] Jesus said, "I am. And you will see the Son of Man seated in the place of power at God's right hand and coming on the clouds of heaven." [63] Then the high priest tore his clothing to show his horror and said, "Why do we need other witnesses? [64] You have all heard his blasphemy. What is your verdict?" "Guilty!" they all cried. "He deserves to die!" [65] Then some of them began to spit at him, and they blindfolded him and beat him with their fists. "Prophesy to us," they jeered. And the guards slapped him as they took him away.

11. **John 10:31-33:** [31] Once again the people picked up stones to kill him. [32] Jesus said, "At my Father's direction I have done many good works. For which one are you going to stone me?" [33] They replied,

85

"We're stoning you not for any good work, but for blasphemy! You, a mere man, claim to be God."

12. **Exodus 3:12-15:** [12] God answered, "I will be with you. And this is your sign that I am the one who has sent you: When you have brought the people out of Egypt, you will worship God at this very mountain." [13] But Moses protested, "If I go to the people of Israel and tell them, 'The God of your ancestors has sent me to you,' they will ask me, 'What is his name?' Then what should I tell them?" [14] God replied to Moses, "I am who i am. Say this to the people of Israel: I am has sent me to you." [15] God also said to Moses, "Say this to the people of Israel: Yahweh, the God of your ancestors - the God of Abraham, the God of Isaac, and the God of Jacob - has sent me to you. This is my eternal name, my name to remember for all generations."

13. **John 8:58-59:** [58] Jesus answered, "I tell you the truth, before Abraham was even born, I am!" [59] At that point they picked up stones to throw at him. But Jesus was hidden from them and left the Temple.

14. **John 6:35:** Jesus replied, "I am the bread of life. Whoever comes to me will never be hungry again. Whoever believes in me will never be thirsty."

15. **John 8:12:** Jesus spoke to the people once more and said, "I am the light of the world. If you follow me, you won't have to walk in darkness, because you will have the light that leads to life."

16. **John 10:7-9:** [7] ...so (Jesus) explained it to them: "I tell you the truth, I am the gate for the sheep. [8] All who came before me were thieves and robbers. But the true sheep did not listen to them [9] Yes, I am the gate. Those who come in through me will be saved. They will come and go freely and will find good pastures."

17. **John 10:11:** (Jesus said) "I am the good shepherd. The good shepherd sacrifices his life for the sheep."

18. **John 15:1:** (Jesus said) "I am the true grapevine, and my Father is the gardener."

19. **John 18:4-6:** [4] Jesus fully realized all that was going to happen to him, so he stepped forward to meet them. "Who are you looking for?" he asked. [5] "Jesus the Nazarene," they replied. "I am he," Jesus said. (Judas, who betrayed him, was standing with them.) [6] As Jesus said "I am he," they all drew back and fell to the ground!

20. **Isaiah 9:6:** For a child is born to us, a son is given to us. The government will rest on his shoulders. And he will be called: Wonderful Counselor, Mighty God, Everlasting Father, Prince of Peace.

21. **Isaiah 11:1-5:** Out of the stump of David's family will grow a shoot - yes, a new Branch bearing fruit from the old root. [2] And the Spirit of the Lord will rest on him the Spirit of wisdom and understanding, the Spirit of counsel and might, the Spirit of knowledge and the fear of the Lord. [3] He will delight in obeying the Lord. He will not judge by appear- ance nor make a decision based on hearsay. [4] He will give justice to the poor and make fair decisions for the exploited. The earth will shake at the force of his word, and one breath from his mouth will destroy the wicked. [5] He will wear righteousness like a belt and truth like an undergarment.

22. **Isaiah 53:** Who has believed our message? To whom has the Lord revealed his powerful arm? [2] My servant grew up in the Lord's presence like a tender green shoot, like a root in dry ground. There was nothing beautiful or majestic about his appearance, nothing to attract us to him. [3] He was despised and rejected - a man of sorrows, acquainted with deepest grief. We turned our backs on him and looked the other way. He was despised, and we did not care. [4] Yet it was our weaknesses he carried; it was our sorrows that weighed him down. And we thought his troubles were a punishment from God, a punishment for his own sins! [5] But he was pierced for our rebellion, crushed for our sins. He was beaten so we could be whole. He was whipped so we could be healed. [6] All of us, like sheep, have strayed away. We have left God's paths to follow our own. Yet the Lord laid

on him the sins of us all. [7] He was oppressed and treated harshly, yet he never said a word. He was led like a lamb to the slaughter. And as a sheep is silent before the shearers, he did not open his mouth. [8] Unjustly condemned, he was led away. No one cared that he died without descendants, that his life was cut short in midstream. But he was struck down for the rebellion of my people. [9] He had done no wrong and had never deceived anyone. But he was buried like a criminal; he was put in a rich man's grave. [10] But it was the Lord's good plan to crush him and cause him grief. Yet when his life is made an offering for sin, he will have many descendants. He will enjoy a long life, and the Lord's good plan will prosper in his hands. [11] When he sees all that is accomplished by his anguish, he will be satisfied. And because of his experience, my righteous servant will make it possible for many to be counted righteous, for he will bear all their sins. [12] I will give him the honors of a victorious soldier, because he exposed himself to death. He was counted among the rebels. He bore the sins of many and interceded for rebels.

23. **Micah 5:2-4:** [2] But you, O Bethlehem Ephrathah, are only a small village among all the people of Judah. Yet a ruler of Israel, whose origins are in the distant past, will come from you on my behalf. [3] The people of Israel will be abandoned to their enemies until the woman in labor gives birth. Then at last his fellow countrymen will return from exile to their own land. [4] And he will stand to lead his flock with the Lord's strength, in the majesty of the name of the Lord his God. Then his people will live there undisturbed, for he will be highly honored around the world.

24. **Colossians 2:9-10:** [9] For in Christ lives all the fullness of God in a human body. [10] So you also are complete through your union with Christ, who is the head over every ruler and authority.

25. **1 Timothy 4:10:** This is why we work hard and continue to struggle, for our hope is in the living God, who is the Savior of all people and particularly of all believers.

26. **2 Pet 1:1:** This letter is from Simon Peter, a slave and apostle of Jesus Christ. I am writing to you who share the same precious faith we have. This faith was given to you because of the justice and fairness of Jesus Christ, our God and Savior.

27. **Isaiah 43:11:** I, yes I, am the Lord, and there is no other Savior.

28. **Titus 2:13-14:** [13] while we look forward with hope to that wonderful day when the glory of our great God and Savior, Jesus Christ, will be revealed. [14] He gave his life to free us from every kind of sin, to cleanse us, and to make us his very own people, totally committed to doing good deeds.

29. **1 Samuel 2:2:** No one is holy like the Lord! There is no one besides you; there is no Rock like our God.

30. **1 Peter 2:5-8:** [5] And you are living stones that God is building into his spiritual temple. What's more, you are his holy priests. Through the mediation of Jesus Christ, you offer spiritual sacrifices that please God. [6] As the Scriptures say, "I am placing a cornerstone in Jerusalem, chosen for great honor, and anyone who trusts in him will never be disgraced." [7] Yes, you who trust him recognize the honor God has given him. But for those who reject him, "The stone that the builders rejected has now become the cornerstone." [8] And, "He is the stone that makes people stumble, the rock that makes them fall." They stumble because they do not obey God's word, and so they meet the fate that was planned for them.

31. **Isaiah 8:14:** He will keep you safe. But to Israel and Judah he will be a stone that makes people stumble, a rock that makes them fall. And for the people of Jerusalem he will be a trap and a snare.

32. **1 Corinthians 10:3-4:** [3] All of them ate the same spiritual food, [4] and all of them drank the same spiritual water. For they drank from the spiritual rock that traveled with them, and that rock was Christ.

33. **Colossians 1:15-20:** [15] Christ is the visible image of the invisible God. He existed before anything was created and is supreme over all

creation, [16] for through him God created everything in the heavenly realms and on earth. He made the things we can see and the things we can't see - such as thrones, kingdoms, rulers, and authorities in the unseen world. Everything was created through him and for him. [17] He existed before anything else, and he holds all creation together. [18] Christ is also the head of the church, which is his body. He is the beginning, supreme over all who rise from the dead. So he is first in everything. [19] For God in all his fullness was pleased to live in Christ, [20] and through him God reconciled everything to himself. He made peace with everything in heaven and on earth by means of Christ's blood on the cross.

34. **1 Timothy 6:15:** For, at just the right time Christ will be revealed from heaven by the blessed and only almighty God, the King of all kings and Lord of all lords.

35. **Hebrews 1:6-12:** [6] And when he brought his supreme Son into the world, God said, "Let all of God's angels worship him." [7] Regarding the angels, he says, "He sends his angels like the winds, his servants like flames of fire." [8] But to the Son he says, "Your throne, O God, endures forever and ever. You rule with a scepter of justice. [9] You love justice and hate evil. Therefore, O God, your God has anointed you, pouring out the oil of joy on you more than on anyone else." [10] He also says to the Son, "In the beginning, Lord, you laid the foundation of the earth and made the heavens with your hands. [11] They will perish, but you remain forever. They will wear out like old clothing. [12] You will fold them up like a cloak and discard them like old clothing. But you are always the same; you will live forever."

36. **1 Corinthians 15:47:** [47] Adam, the first man, was made from the dust of the earth, while Christ, the second man, came from heaven.

37. **Hebrews 7:24-28:** [24] But because Jesus lives forever, his priesthood lasts forever. [25] Therefore he is able, once and forever, to save those who come to God through him. He lives forever to intercede with God on their behalf. [26] He is the kind of high priest we need because he

is holy and blameless, unstained by sin. He has been set apart from sinners and has been given the highest place of honor in heaven. [27] Unlike those other high priests, he does not need to offer sacrifices every day. They did this for their own sins first and then for the sins of the people. But Jesus did this once for all when he offered himself as the sacrifice for the people's sins. [28] The law appointed high priests who were limited by human weakness. But after the law was given, God appointed his Son with an oath, and his Son has been made the perfect High Priest forever.

38. **Romans 8:34:** Who then will condemn us? No one - for Christ Jesus died for us and was raised to life for us, and he is sitting in the place of honor at God's right hand, pleading for us.

39. **1 Peter 1:18-20:** [18] For you know that God paid a ransom to save you from the empty life you inherited from your ancestors. And it was not paid with mere gold or silver, which lose their value. [19] It was the precious blood of Christ, the sinless, spotless Lamb of God. [20] God chose him as your ransom long before the world began, but now in these last days he has been revealed for your sake.

40. **1 Peter 2:22-25:** He never sinned, nor ever deceived anyone. [23] He did not retaliate when he was insulted, nor threaten revenge when he suffered. He left his case in the hands of God, who always judges fairly. [24] He personally carried our sins in his body on the cross so that we can be dead to sin and live for what is right. By his wounds you are healed. [25] Once you were like sheep who wandered away. But now you have turned to your Shepherd, the Guardian of your souls.

41. **1 John 3:5:** [5] And you know that Jesus came to take away our sins, and there is no sin in him.

42. **Philippians 2:6-11:** [6] Though he was God, he did not think of equality with God as something to cling to. [7] Instead, he gave up his divine privileges; he took the humble position of a slave and was born as a human being. When he appeared in human form, [8] he humbled himself in obedience to God and died a criminal's death on

a cross. [9] Therefore, God elevated him to the place of highest honor and gave him the name above all other names, [10] that at the name of Jesus every knee should bow, in heaven and on earth and under the earth, [11] and every tongue declare that Jesus Christ is Lord, to the glory of God the Father.

43. **2 Corinthians 5:10:** For we must all stand before Christ to be judged. We will each receive whatever we deserve for the good or evil we have done in this earthly body.

44. **Romans 9:5b:** And he (Jesus) is God, the one who rules over everything and is worthy of eternal praise! Amen.

45. **Revelation 1:5:** ...[5] and from Jesus Christ. He is the faithful witness to these things, the first to rise from the dead, and the ruler of all the kings of the world. All glory to him who loves us and has freed us from our sins by shedding his blood for us.

46. **Ephesians 1:21:** [21] Now he (Jesus) is far above any ruler or authority or power or leader or anything else - not only in this world but also in the world to come.

47. **Revelation 19:11-16:** [11] Then I saw heaven opened, and a white horse was standing there. Its rider was named Faithful and True, for he judges fairly and wages a righteous war. [12] His eyes were like flames of fire, and on his head were many crowns. A name was written on him that no one understood except himself. [13] He wore a robe dipped in blood, and his title was the Word of God. [14] The armies of heaven, dressed in the finest of pure white linen, followed him on white horses. [15] From his mouth came a sharp sword to strike down the nations. He will rule them with an iron rod. He will release the fierce wrath of God, the Almighty, like juice flowing from a winepress. [16] On his robe at his thigh was written this title: King of all kings and Lord of all lords.

48. **John 14:6-9b:** [6] Jesus told him, "I am the way, the truth, and the life. No one can come to the Father except through me. [7] If you had really

known me, you would know who my Father is. From now on, you do know him and have seen him!" [8] Philip said, "Lord, show us the Father, and we will be satisfied." [9] Jesus replied, "Have I been with you all this time, Philip, and yet you still don't know who I am? Anyone who has seen me has seen the Father!"

WHO IS THE HOLY SPIRIT?

The Holy Spirit is probably the most misunderstood and unfamiliar Person of the Triune Godhead. Part of the problem is that He is not often taught of in many churches, so a great "mystery" surrounds Him. At other times, the Holy Spirit is misused, and this can create an uncomfortable atmosphere for those who are seeking God.

People often shy away from things they don't understand, so a natural tendency may be to ignore or to evade the Holy Spirit. But since Scripture has much to say about Him, especially in the New Testament, we need to take steps to search Him out, to meet Him, and to access His power so we can live a victorious Christian life. Scripture says that we *must* know and be intimate with the Holy Spirit IF we want a vital, successful relationship with the Lord (Rom 8: 5-8[1]).

One very important point that needs to be addressed as we begin our study is that we are not to make the Holy Spirit our *main* focus or to elevate Him. Some people do this, and they end up with phenomena like "The Laughter Movement", with people rolling around on the floor in church. Also, I have witnessed some folks who "speak loudly in tongues" in an assembly, but with no order or unity. This generally does not edify God at all. When the Spirit of God is abused in this way, it can actually lead people *away* from Jesus.

At the other end of the spectrum are those who are so afraid of the Spirit, they shut Him out. They may feel a little nudge during the service to have an alter call or to tarry for a moment after a particularly moving song, but they squash that unction, for fear their emotions may spin out of control. The sad result is that many churches today run on autopilot – just 'doing' church. It's the same old routine week after week, with little joy, peace, or real unity from the Spirit taking place.

So Let's Find Out Who This Beautiful Person Is

The Holy Spirit Is God Himself

We find that in the very beginning, before time began or the earth was formed, the Holy Spirit *hovered* over the surface of the waters (Genesis 1:1-2[2]). In other translations, the word "hover" is also called "moved". What is so interesting is that this word "moved" is used in the Bible approximately 74 times, but there is only one Hebrew word for this particular meaning in all of Scripture. Its root word is *rachaph* (pronounced 'raw- coff'), which means "to brood", "to be relaxed", "to flutter", "to move", or "to shake".

The Bible also tells us the Holy Spirit is Co-Creator of the universe, along with the Father and the Son, Jesus (Genesis 1:26[3] and Job 33:4[4]). "Us" in this Genesis account is the Triune Godhead speaking to Themselves! This signifies that the Holy Spirit is Eternal; not only was He active in the Creation, but we know that only God can create something out of nothing.

The Holy Spirit is also able to give life, which describes the Deity, or Divinity of the Holy Spirit, because only God can create and sustain life (Deuteronomy 32:39[5]; 1 Samuel 2:6[6]). We also see the Spirit's unique power throughout Scripture, such as raising people from the dead (Romans 8:11[7])!

There are many scriptural accounts of God, Jesus and the Holy Spirit having the same traits and power. Jesus and the Holy Spirit have many identical names and roles. Even as the Holy Spirit is co-creator, we find this true of Christ (Colossians 1:15-20[8]). This validates the God-status and the Eternality (the state of having no beginning and no ending) of the Father, the Son, **and** the Holy Spirit, because again, only GOD can create.

Don't forget from our previous studies that to attribute the same power, authority, and majesty to anyone *except* God is blasphemy. Indeed, the Holy Spirit is literally called "God" in Acts 5:3-4[9]. Peter is telling Ananias that he lied to the Holy Spirit – and in the same sentence, he says "You were lying to GOD".

The Holy Spirit Is A Person

Since the Holy Spirit is *Spirit*, we often fail to see Him as a Person. But in reality, we can envision Him in the same way we do our Father God, because He is also Spirit (John 4:23-24[10]). We may tend to focus only on the Father and Jesus, but this discounts a third of the Personhood of the Trinity. And this severely debilitates our faith! The fact is, we desperately need the Holy Spirit, because He imparts Truth, Comfort, Guidance, Conviction, and Power to our lives. And this is the **only way** we can possibly live the life that Jesus calls us to.

We can only live a holy life by the power of God. So, after Christ paid our sin-debt and ascended back into heaven, He imparted His Spirit to His followers so they would have the power, the direction, the wisdom, the boldness, and the strength to live righteously.

In the Old Testament, the Holy Spirit was still very active, but His power was usually only manifest in select people, for certain times and events. In the Jewish culture, God was not thought of as a Friend or a Father, but a faraway, altogether separate, absolutely Holy, unable-to-approach Deity.

In the New Testament, we read of the supernatural act of God as His Spirit personally came to live within His followers. This event was called "Pentecost". 'Pente', in the word *Pente*cost, is the Greek word for "fifty" and this amazing occurrence happened fifty days after Passover – which was, in fact, the day before Jesus was crucified (Acts 2:1-21[11]).

To think that God (the Father) would come near to us, live as one of us, and would die for us (God the Son, Jesus), and that He would even *live INSIDE of us* (God the Holy Spirit), was *unthinkable!* What we take for granted today was unfathomable then.

What's really interesting is that Pentecost was originally an Old Testament festival. Fifty days (literally 49 days – seven full weeks) after Passover, the Jews would celebrate "The Feast of Harvest", also called "The Feast of Weeks". God's people would bring their offerings of grain to Him and praise Him for the harvest (Deuteronomy 16:9-10[12]).

The Feast of Harvest is one of the only Old Testament festivals still in effect today, because most of the old festivals were centered around the sacrificial system – the shedding of animal blood for sin - which Jesus abolished when He became the Sacrificial Lamb who died on the cross. However, Jews who have not believed on the Lord Jesus Christ for salvation today may still practice all of the old festivals, because they don't believe the Messiah has come yet.

Presently, the Feast of Harvest – Pentecost - is a fitting New Testament celebration, for the Holy Spirit is the One who brings a "harvest" of right living into our lives, and He helps us to "harvest" souls for Christ. And Pentecost allows us a time of reflection and thankfulness for God's provision and work in our lives.

Functions Of The Holy Spirit

The Holy Spirit imparts many wonderful and important gifts to those who have entrusted their lives to Jesus. The Spirit is the primary influence in our spiritual, mental, emotional, and physical lives after we receive salvation. It is His responsibility to continually guide us, lead us, empower us, and direct us all of our days, **as** we remain united with Christ. The words "entrusted" and "remain" in this paragraph imply an honest, consistent, and intimate commitment that we have to God *if* we are to receive His power and blessings.

In John 14: 9-11[13], Jesus says that He and the Father are One. He is stating here that they are equal! Not only that, but the Spirit is also One with the Father and the Son. That's why we say "In the Name of the Father, the Son, and the Holy Spirit". Since only God can be completely in harmony and unity with Himself, this attributes Godhood status to the Holy Spirit – identical in power and glory with the Father and the Son.

One of the greatest gifts the Holy Spirit gives us is spiritual birth (John 3:5-8[14]; Titus 3:4-6[15]). He also gives us Eternal Life (John 6:63[16]). Let's look at John 14:17[17]. Notice that Jesus says "You know Him (The Holy Spirit) because He lives *with* you now", but He doesn't say "*in*" you now. Remember, the Holy Spirit wasn't unleashed personally into Christians' lives until after Jesus' death, burial, resurrection, and the subsequent Pentecost (John 7:39[18]).

Don't forget that the Holy Spirit comes *into us* at the moment of salvation – by baptizing us *spiritually.* At that time, He fills us with Himself (Acts 1:5-8[19]). We are also physically and spiritually baptized into Jesus

Christ, as a public witness of our salvation and the gift of our eternal life (Acts 2:38[20]; John 6:27[21]).

Let's look again at John 14:17c[22] ("c" is the third sentence in one Scripture verse). It says that the Spirit was *here with them now* – because He was living in and through Jesus, who was physically with the disciples. But this passage goes on to say that "He (the Spirit) would be later be IN them". This is more evidence that Jesus and the Spirit were One, because when Jesus says that HE is with us, then the Holy Spirit is with us.

Furthermore, John 14:18[23] says that *Jesus will* 'come to us'. Remember, Jesus isn't coming back in literal, physical form until the Second Coming in the future. So He was speaking of "coming to the believer" in the form of the Holy Spirit.

In fact, Jesus tells us He left the earth specifically *so that the Holy Spirit could come to us* (John 16:7[24]). This is because Jesus was unable to reach the whole world *as a man*, but the Spirit of God can personally live in every person who decides to accept Jesus as their Lord and Savior. And what's even more amazing is that Jesus says YOU AND I – His followers - will be one with the Father, Son and Holy Spirit (John 14:20[25])!

Other Attributes Of The Remarkable Spirit of God

The Holy Spirit is our Advocate. What's so precious is that the title *Advocate* is also attributed to Jesus (1 John 2:1[26]). An advocate is someone who stands up for those who are weaker or less experienced, defending their position. Given our sinful nature and the vulnerability to our enemy, Satan, we are in desperate need of great strength and support. We need someone who will fight for us and protect us, someone who isn't limited by human frailty.

Furthermore, the Holy Spirit is called the Spirit of Truth, and He guides us into all truth (John 16:13a[27]). Jesus is also called the Truth (John 14:6[28]). And the Bible says that God cannot lie (because He is Truth) *parenthesis mine* (Heb 6:18[29]). Oftentimes, when we hear the word *truth,* we think of "telling the truth", something we may or may not do at any given time. But the Members of the Trinity ARE Truth. They embody truth, and they cannot help but be truthful 100% of the time.

Another exquisite role of the Holy Spirit is that He prays for us and intercedes for us (Romans 8:26-27[30]). This is also something Jesus does for us (Hebrews 7:24-25[31]). Finally, the Beautiful Holy Spirit is also our Teacher (1 John 2:26-27[32]). And interestingly, Jesus is also called our Teacher in John 13:13[33].

So, to highlight Who the Lovely Holy Spirit is:

He is the third part of the Triune Godhead (Father, Son, and Holy Spirit). He is the Co-Creator of the universe. He convicts us of sin.

He opens unbelievers' spiritual eyes. He convinces us of our need for salvation. He confirms the Truth of God's Word. He guarantees our salvation and right standing with God when we genuinely commit our lives to Jesus Christ.

The Holy Spirit also:

- Gives us our faith
- Imparts the power we need to live according to God's desires
- Ends our bondage to evil desires
- Creates fruit in us, as described in Galatians 5:22-23[34]
- Is a wonderful, wise, and loving Counselor
- Helps us and comforts us in our time of need

We can only live a godly life by concentrating on our relationship with Jesus. We accomplish this through daily prayer; Bible study; genuine, repentant, and heartfelt confession; and fellowship with other authentic believers. But the POWER to live this kind of life comes only from the Holy Spirit. Our job is to give Him permission to make the necessary changes in us, and to obey His leading and instruction. The Holy Spirit longs for us to experience the freedom that God intended for our lives. He wants us to become more like Jesus, so we can bring glory to the Father. And He desires for us to fulfill our Christian role of bringing others into the Kingdom of God.

The Holy Spirit is the One Who gives the Christian life vitality!

CHAPTER 8
Scripture Verses

1. **Rom 8:5-8:** Those who are dominated by the sinful nature think about sinful things, but those who are controlled by the Holy Spirit think about things that please the Spirit. [6] So letting your sinful nature control your mind leads to death. But letting the Spirit control your mind leads to life and peace. [7] For the sinful nature is always hostile to God. It never did obey God's laws, and it never will. [8] That's why those who are still under the control of their sinful nature can never please God.

2. **Genesis 1:1-2:** In the beginning God created the heavens and the earth. [2] The earth was formless and empty, and darkness covered the deep waters. And the Spirit of God was hovering over the surface of the waters.

3. **Genesis 1:26:** Then God said, "Let us make human beings in our image, to be like us. They will reign over the fish in the sea, the birds in the sky, the livestock, all the wild animals on the earth, and the small animals that scurry along the ground."

4. **Job 33:4:** For the Spirit of God has made me, and the breath of the Almighty gives me life.

5. **Deuteronomy 32:39:** Look now; I myself am he! There is no other god but me! I am the one who kills and gives life; I am the one who wounds and heals; no one can be rescued from my powerful hand!

6. **1 Samuel 2:6:** The Lord gives both death and life; he brings some down to the grave but raises others up.

7. **Romans 8:11:** The Spirit of God, who raised Jesus from the dead, lives in you. And just as God raised Christ Jesus from the dead, he will give life to your mortal bodies by this same Spirit living within you.

8. **Colossians 1:15-20:** Christ is the visible image of the invisible God. He existed before anything was created and is supreme over all

creation, [16] for through him God created everything in the heavenly realms and on earth. He made the things we can see and the things we can't see - such as thrones, kingdoms, rulers, and authorities in the unseen world. Everything was created through him and for him. [17] He existed before anything else, and he holds all creation together. [18] Christ is also the head of the church, which is his body. He is the beginning, supreme over all who rise from the dead. So he is first in everything. [19] For God in all his fullness was pleased to live in Christ, and through him God reconciled everything to himself. He made peace with everything in heaven and on earth by means of Christ's blood on the cross.

9. **Acts 5:3-4:** Then Peter said, "Ananias, why have you let Satan fill your heart? You lied to the Holy Spirit, and you kept some of the money for yourself. [4] The property was yours to sell or not sell, as you wished. And after selling it, the money was also yours to give away. How could you do a thing like this? You weren't lying to us but to God!"

10. **John 4:23-24:** "But the time is coming - indeed it's here now—when true worshipers will worship the Father in spirit and in truth. The Father is looking for those who will worship him that way. [24] For God is Spirit, so those who worship him must worship in spirit and in truth."

11. **Acts 2:1-21:** On the day of Pentecost, all the believers were meeting together in one place. [2] Suddenly, there was a sound from heaven like the roaring of a mighty windstorm, and it filled the house where they were sitting. [3] Then, what looked like flames or tongues of fire appeared and settled on each of them. [4] And everyone present was filled with the Holy Spirit and began speaking in other languages, as the Holy Spirit gave them this ability. [5] At that time there were devout Jews from every nation living in Jerusalem. [6] When they heard the loud noise, everyone came running, and they were bewildered to hear their own languages being spoken by the believers. [7] They were completely amazed. "How can this be?" they exclaimed. "These people are all from Galilee, [8] and yet we hear them speaking in our

own native languages! [9] Here we are - Parthians, Medes, Elamites, people from Mesopotamia, Judea, Cappadocia, Pontus, the province of Asia, [10] Phrygia, Pamphylia, Egypt, and the areas of Libya around Cyrene, visitors from Rome [11] (both Jews and converts to Judaism), Cretans, and Arabs. And we all hear these people speaking in our own languages about the wonderful things God has done!" [12] They stood there amazed and perplexed. "What can this mean?" they asked each other. [13] But others in the crowd ridiculed them, saying, "They're just drunk, that's all!" [14] Then Peter stepped forward with the eleven other apostles and shouted to the crowd, "Listen carefully, all of you, fellow Jews and residents of Jerusalem! Make no mistake about this. [15] These people are not drunk, as some of you are assuming. Nine o'clock in the morning is much too early for that. [16] No, what you see was predicted long ago by the prophet Joel: [17] 'In the last days,' God says, 'I will pour out my Spirit upon all people. Your sons and daughters will prophesy. Your young men will see visions, and your old men will dream dreams. [18] In those days I will pour out my Spirit even on my servants - men and women alike and they will prophesy. [19] And I will cause wonders in the heavens above and signs on the earth below - blood and fire and clouds of smoke. [20] The sun will become dark, and the moon will turn blood red before that great and glorious day of the Lord arrives. [21] But everyone who calls on the name of the Lord will be saved.'

12. **Deuteronomy 16:9-10:** "Count off seven weeks from when you first begin to cut the grain at the time of harvest. [10] Then celebrate the Festival of Harvest to honor the Lord your God. Bring him a voluntary offering in proportion to the blessings you have received from him."

13. **John 14: 9-11:** Jesus replied, "Have I been with you all this time, Philip, and yet you still don't know who I am? Anyone who has seen me has seen the Father! So why are you asking me to show him to you? [10] Don't you believe that I am in the Father and the Father is in me? The words I speak are not my own, but my Father who lives in me does his work through me. [11] Just believe that I am in the Father

and the Father is in me. Or at least believe because of the work you have seen me do."

14. **John 3:5-8:** Jesus replied, "I assure you, no one can enter the Kingdom of God without being born of water and the Spirit. ⁶ Humans can reproduce only human life, but the Holy Spirit gives birth to spiritual life. ⁷ So don't be surprised when I say, 'You must be born again.' ⁸ The wind blows wherever it wants. Just as you can hear the wind but can't tell where it comes from or where it is going, so you can't explain how people are born of the Spirit."

15. **Titus 3:4-6:** But when God our Savior revealed his kindness and love, ⁵ he saved us, not because of the righteous things we had done, but because of his mercy. He washed away our sins, giving us a new birth and new life through the Holy Spirit. ⁶ He generously poured out the Spirit upon us through Jesus Christ our Savior.

16. **John 6:63:** The Spirit alone gives eternal life. Human effort accomplishes nothing. And the very words I have spoken to you are spirit and life.

17. **John 14:17:** He is the Holy Spirit, who leads into all truth. The world cannot receive him, because it isn't looking for him and doesn't recognize him. But you know him, because he lives with you now and later will be in you.

18. **John 7:39:** (When he said "living water," he was speaking of the Spirit, who would be given to everyone believing in him. But the Spirit had not yet been given, because Jesus had not yet entered into his glory.)

19. **Acts 1:5-8:** "John baptized with water, but in just a few days you will be baptized with the Holy Spirit." ⁶ So when the apostles were with Jesus, they kept asking him, "Lord, has the time come for you to free Israel and restore our kingdom?" ⁷ He replied, "The Father alone has the authority to set those dates and times, and they are not for you to know. ⁸ But you will receive power when the Holy Spirit comes upon you. And you will be my witnesses, telling people about me

everywhere -in Jerusalem, throughout Judea, in Samaria, and to the ends of the earth."

20. **Acts 2:38:** Peter replied, "Each of you must repent of your sins and turn to God, and be baptized in the name of Jesus Christ for the forgiveness of your sins. Then you will receive the gift of the Holy Spirit."

21. **John 6:27:** But don't be so concerned about perishable things like food. Spend your energy seeking the eternal life that the Son of Man can give you. For God the Father has given me the seal of his approval.

22. **John 14:17c:** But you know him, because he lives with you now and later will be in you.

23. **John 14:18:** (Jesus said) "No, I will not abandon you as orphans—I will come to you".

24. **John 16:7:** But in fact, it is best for you that I go away, because if I don't, the Advocate won't come. If I do go away, then I will send him to you.

25. **John 14:20:** When I am raised to life again, you will know that I am in my Father, and you are in me, and I am in you.

26. **1 John 2:1:** My dear children, I am writing this to you so that you will not sin. But if anyone does sin, we have an advocate who pleads our case before the Father. He is Jesus Christ, the one who is truly righteous.

27. **John 16:13a:** When the Spirit of truth comes, he will guide you into all truth.

28. **John 14:6:** Jesus told him, "I am the way, the truth, and the life. No one can come to the Father except through me."

29. **Hebrews 6:18:** So God has given both his promise and his oath. These two things are unchangeable because it is impossible for God to lie. Therefore, we who have fled to him for refuge can have great confidence as we hold to the hope that lies before us.

30. **Romans 8:26-27:** And the Holy Spirit helps us in our weakness. For example, we don't know what God wants us to pray for. But the Holy Spirit prays for us with groanings that cannot be expressed in words. [27] And the Father who knows all hearts knows what the Spirit is saying, for the Spirit pleads for us believers in harmony with God's own will.

31. **Hebrews 7:24-25:** But because Jesus lives forever, his priesthood lasts forever. [25] Therefore he is able, once and forever, to save those who come to God through him. He lives forever to intercede with God on their behalf.

32. **1 John 2:26-27:** I am writing these things to warn you about those who want to lead you astray. [27] But you have received the Holy Spirit, and he lives within you, so you don't need anyone to teach you what is true. For the Spirit teaches you everything you need to know, and what he teaches is true - it is not a lie. So, just as he has taught you, remain in fellowship with Christ.

33. **John 13:13:** You call me 'Teacher' and 'Lord,' and you are right, because that's what I am.

34. **Galatians 5:22-23:** But the Holy Spirit produces this kind of fruit in our lives: love, joy, peace, patience, kindness, goodness, faithfulness, [23] gentleness, and self-control. There is no law against these things!

CHAPTER NINE
WHO IS SATAN?

Most people are curious about Satan. It's generally thought that he's the "bad guy" and God is the "good guy". Some people doubt his existence altogether. Or they think he's the little red cartoon character with a pitchfork. But unless we read the truth of who he is in the Bible, we probably don't have accurate knowledge. He is very real, very evil, and very dangerous.

It may come as a surprise to you that Satan had his beginning in heaven (Isaiah 14: 12-17[1]; Ezekiel 28:12-17[2]). Although these passages were referring Old Testament kings, most Bible scholars attribute them to Satan as well.

Satan was one of the most beautiful of God's creations. He was an angel of great power. Another name for him was *Lucifer,* which means "sense of brightness", or "bright morning star". However, we read in these accounts that he became proud of his beauty and decided to defy the Most High God. His pride caused him to change from a beautiful and beloved angel to being called "The Father of Lies" and "The Ancient Serpent" (John 8:44[3]; Revelation 12:9[4])!

In fact, one of the ways he tries to gain access to human lives is to *disguise himself* as an angel of light. He knows if we realized how evil and hideous he really is, we would have nothing to do with him. And the devil's human followers often conceal their intentions, as well (2 Corinthians 11:12-15[5]). However, this often makes it difficult to distinguish between good and evil, which is why we desperately need discernment from the

Holy Spirit and the Word of God. *Discernment* is the ability to recognize if someone is genuine or counterfeit; truthful or deceitful.

Jesus tells us that He watched Satan fall from heaven (Luke 10:17-18[6]). And since then, Satan has been the very essence of evil, causing destruction upon the earth (1 John 3:8[7]). Actually, Jesus came for the very purpose of freeing people from the devil's clutches (Colossians 1:13-14[8]).

Indeed, the apostle Peter actually reveals one of the main purposes the Lord has for our lives: "But you (Christians) are a chosen race, a holy nation, a people for God's own possession, so that you may proclaim the excellencies of Him (Jesus) who has called you out of darkness (Satan's realm) into His marvelous light (God's Kingdom)" (2 Peter 1:9, NASB; *parenthesis mine*).

The very name "Satan" means *adversary*, which is to be "against" something or someone. He has been against God and everything He stands for since he was thrown down from heaven. He knows he can't fight God directly, so he wars against God's people instead, accusing them day and night (Zechariah 3:1-2[9]; Revelation 12:10[10]). Although much of the evil we see in the world is because of the selfishness of man, many events and situations are worsened because of Satan's work.

Why Is Satan So Successful?

Satan HATES God and His people, and his evil plan is to kill, maim, and destroy whatever and whomever God loves (John 10:10[11]). He despises mankind in general, because we all were created in the image of God. But he has a special, vehement hatred towards those who love Jesus.

He will try every device at his disposal to get us off track and to take our focus away from God. It is foolish to deny that he is immeasurably more powerful than we are. And as a master counterfeiter, he loves nothing more than when people believe he doesn't exist. We must believe Satan is real!

One of the main ways the devil operates is to cast doubt in our minds, tempting us to turn from God and His truth. We see this in the famous account of Adam and Eve. They were told by God not to eat of the tree of good and evil, but the serpent (Satan) put it in Eve's mind that there was a whole lot she was missing out on, and that God was selfishly holding it back from her. So *she believed the devil instead of God*, and the results were utterly catastrophic (Genesis 3:1-24[12]).

By this account, we see that Satan is able to interject thoughts into our minds, although he is unable to "read our minds". He watches our behavior, though, and he knows our weaknesses. Interestingly, Satan still uses this tactic of planting doubt today, and it still causes millions of people to stray from God and His plans.

Satan's Limited Power

Satan is allowed access to God Himself. He is also permitted to tempt God's people, who are called "believers" (Job 1:1-12[13]). But thankfully, Christians have Jesus protecting them and praying for them to overcome these tests (Luke 22:31-32[14]). However, if you are not in relationship with God through salvation in Jesus Christ, you cannot expect the same protection from the devil. Unbelievers (those who are not saved) can actually have their souls possessed by Satan. That means he can literally take over the mind and will of a human being (Luke 22:3[15]).

Again, it is impossible for genuine believers to be possessed by Satan, because the Holy Spirit lives within them, and the devil cannot co-exist with God. But Satan can still create havoc and *oppress* the believer (Acts 10:38[16]; 1 Thessalonians 2:18[17]; 1 Peter 5:8-9[18]). God may even allow the devil and his demons to create hardship in our lives to cause us to lean on Him more fully and build our character (2 Corinthians 12:7b[19]).

Some manifestations of satanic possession are mental disorders (Mark 5:1-15[20]). The Bible also records demonic activity in the form of violent acts (Luke 8:26-29[21]), and bodily disease or impairment (Luke 13:11[22]; Matthew 12:22[23]). Obviously, this doesn't mean that when people get sick, act violently, or have mental illness that they are possessed by the devil! But this can certainly be a contributing factor.

Satan also has a great army of fallen angels, who are called *demons.* Another of Satan's titles is *Beelzebub,* which means "chief of evil spirits" or "prince of demons "(Matthew 12:24[24]). Although this particular Scripture is referring to the Pharisee's hatred of Jesus and implication that His power was from the devil, this passage was used to show that Satan is called "The prince of demons".

Since Satan is a created being, he cannot be everywhere at once. Only God Himself is "omnipresent" which means everywhere at the same time. So Satan uses his demons to do his dirty work for him. In fact, demons have territories, or geographical areas, they are responsible for (Daniel 10:13[25]; Ephesians 6:10-12[26]).

Satan is called "the god of this world" and "the ruler of this world" (Luke 4:5-6[27]; John 12:31[28]; 2 Corinthians 4:3-4[29]; 1 John 5:19[30]). The *world* in this context is the material, societal, economic, political, and physical realm that humans live in. That is why you see so much evil amongst people who don't have faith in Jesus. Their minds are literally controlled by the devil (Ephesians 2:1-2[31]).

Even Christians obeyed the devil before accepting Jesus. But they made the crucial, eternal decision to reject the enemy of their souls and turn instead to Jesus, the Lover of their souls. It is imperative to understand that it is your choice alone as to whom you will serve. Notice the following Scripture mentions only false gods, and "The Lord" – either - or (Joshua 24:15[32]).

Whom Will You Serve?

Just as God is Truth and therefore, He cannot lie, Satan is a liar and a murderer at his very core. And just as people can choose to imitate and reflect the character of God, they can also imitate and reflect the character of Satan (2 Timothy 2:25-26[33]). It is everyone's personal choice as to whom they will dedicate their life. The truth is, you will either choose to follow Jesus, or you will choose to follow the enemy of your soul (Matthew 12:30[34]).

The Bible clearly states it is one's *overall lifestyle* of righteousness or sinfulness that separates believers from unbelievers (1 John 3:9-10[35]). As Christians, we will obviously make mistakes! Don't forget – our "righteousness" comes from Jesus, not by our efforts. But you alone can make the choice to "live" on one side or the other, according to your motives, thoughts, and actions.

You may think to yourself: "I don't follow Jesus, but I'm not a devil worshiper!" However, we cannot be neutral. We are either living in the darkness or living in the light – living for Satan or living for Christ (Acts

26:15-18[36]). Satan's only motive is to enslave and destroy us. **Only** Christ can set us free – because He is the only one who has the desire and the power to do so.

Our choice to love Jesus or to reject Him is what we will be judged for in the end. There is no middle ground; we can't "sort of" be a Christian. In fact, God hates this hypocritical behavior. He would rather you just deny Him upfront rather than pretend to be a Christian (Revelation 3:15-16[37])!

New believers are especially vulnerable to Satan's attacks (Luke 8:12[38]), and that's why it is essential that they are trained directly after salvation to learn Christian doctrine. They need those who are mature in the faith to help them understand how to withstand the assaults of the devil, how to pray, how to overcome their old desires, and how to read the Word of God.

How Should We Deal With Satan?

My personal belief is that we should not communicate with the devil in any way. I have witnessed some Christians engaging in conversation with him, yelling at him, and demanding him to obey them! I actually looked up the words "yelling and screaming" in the Bible – I only found yelling mentioned when it was happening between people. And "screaming" is only recorded as it relates to *demons* when they come up against Jesus and a couple of demon possessed men!

Instead of having anything to do with Satan, I prefer to go to my Lord and ask for protection, and to ask HIM to fight my battles against my enemy. Even Michael the Archangel asked the Lord to deal with Satan (Jude 1:9[39]).

Finally, we are to resolutely stay away from *anything* that has to do with the occult. This includes fortune telling, ouiji boards, horoscopes, séances, and mediums (Deuteronomy 18:9-14[40]; Isaiah 8:19[41]). What may seem like an innocent pastime can literally enslave you. Satan is a cruel taskmaster and he will stop at nothing to take you out. Everything we need to know about the devil – our foe – is in the Bible. *God* wants to be the One who gives us wisdom and direction.

The Bible tells believers to *resist* the devil – and he will flee - which means to leave in a great hurry (James 4:7[42])! But first, we must humble ourselves and submit our lives to God. Only **then** we will be able to withstand the devil's onslaughts. God wants our entire being – our heart, our mind, our soul, and our body – to be under His loving control.

As we live in deep and daily communion with the Lord, we are afforded protection from Satan. Of course, as previously mentioned, we will still have problems and we may even continue to be harassed by that lying serpent! But living life our own way and then saying a quick prayer to get us out of trouble is not going to bring us real security!

This is why God has given us spiritual weapons for this spiritual war. These weapons are supernatural, and they will only be effective as they are used regularly, and in the power of the Holy Spirit. The mightiest weapons we use against the devil are the Word of God – which is called "The Sword of the Spirit" - and prayer.

Other weapons of our warfare are listed in Ephesians 6:13-18[43]. Notice this passage doesn't tell us to go out and fight, or to yell at, or to try to take down the enemy. We are commanded to STAND FIRM. The only offensive weapon listed is the Bible, and we can read and speak Scripture when we are under attack.

I Thought I Saw A Miracle!

In the days leading up to the physical and visible Second Coming of Jesus Christ, people will sense the end drawing near. There will be more natural disasters and greater evil. Even people who claim to follow Christ will reject Him. This is a recipe for widespread deception. People will be searching for answers, and they will accept many false ideas and methods to alleviate their fears and insecurities. Enter: The Last Assault of Satan.

In the last days, miracles will increase, which is why we have to be very careful about supernatural activity (2 Thessalonians 2:9-10[44]; Revelation 16:14[45]). These Scriptures are speaking of the Antichrist – the one who will come at the end of time to deceive and destroy everyone in his path, and will be empowered by Satan. But be aware that Satan and his demons are able to perform miracles even now.

Again, just because we see a miracle doesn't always mean it's from God (Revelation 19:20[46]). The devil will use these counterfeit methods to try to lead people away from the Lord. In fact, he will even *be given* power by God to resurrect someone from the dead (Revelation 13:11-15[47]). The fantastic news is that Satan and his demons will eventually be cast into the lake of sulfur and fire to suffer forever and ever (Revelation 20:7-10[48]). The greatest sorrow, however, will be for those who refuse God's offer of salvation through Jesus Christ while they are alive on earth. They will join the devil in the burning lake that was originally intended only for the devil and his demons (Matthew 25:41[49]).

Once we die, there is no changing our minds. The decision to follow God - or the devil – and therefore, to live in heaven or hell - is made only in this lifetime. That is why it is so essential for Christians to lovingly share their faith with everyone possible, as they are led by the Holy Spirit. Satan and hell are very real. You *will* live eternally – but only *you* can choose your eternal destination. And only God, through Jesus Christ, can make our paths straight and give us victory to overcome so we can live with Him forever (Proverbs 3:5-6[50]; 4:10-13[51]).

Fight the devil by determining to serve Jesus Christ with your whole life!

CHAPTER 9
Scripture Verses

1.   **Isaiah 14:12-17:** [12] "How you are fallen from heaven, O shining star, son of the morning! You have been thrown down to the earth, you who destroyed the nations of the world. [13] For you said to yourself, 'I will ascend to heaven and set my throne above God's stars. I will preside on the mountain of the gods far away in the north. [14] I will climb to the highest heavens and be like the Most High.' [15] Instead, you will be brought down to the place of the dead, down to its lowest depths. [16] Everyone there will stare at you and ask 'Can this be the one who shook the earth and made the kingdoms of the world tremble? [17] Is this the one who destroyed the world and made it into a wasteland? Is this the king who demolished the world's greatest cities and had no mercy on his prisoners?'

2.   **Ezekiel 28:12-17:** [12] "Son of man, sing this funeral song for the king of Tyre. Give him this message from the Sovereign Lord:"You were the model of perfection, full of wisdom and exquisite in beauty. [13] You were in Eden, the garden of God. Your clothing was adorned with every precious stone; red carnelian, pale-green peridot, white moonstone, blue-green beryl, onyx, green jasper, blue lapis lazuli, turquoise, and emerald, all beautifully crafted for you and set in the finest gold. They were given to you on the day you were created. [14] I ordained and anointed you as the mighty angelic guardian. You had access to the holy mountain of God and walked among the stones of fire. [15] "You were blameless in all you did from the day you were created until the day evil was found in you. [16] Your rich commerce led you to violence, and you sinned. So I banished you in disgrace from the mountain of God. I expelled you, O mighty guardian, from your place among the stones of fire. [17] Your heart was filled with pride because of all your beauty. Your wisdom was corrupted by your love of splendor. So I threw you to the ground and exposed you to the curious gaze of kings."

3. **John 8:44:** For you are the children of your father the devil, and you love to do the evil things he does. He was a murderer from the beginning. He has always hated the truth, because there is no truth in him. When he lies, it is consistent with his character; for he is a liar and the father of lies.

4. **Revelation 12:9:** This great dragon—the ancient serpent called the devil, or Satan, the one deceiving the whole world—was thrown down to the earth with all his angels.

5. **2 Corinthians 11:12-15:** [12] But I will continue doing what I have always done. This will undercut those who are looking for an opportunity to boast that their work is just like ours. [13] These people are false apostles. They are deceitful workers who disguise themselves as apostles of Christ. [14] But I am not surprised! Even Satan disguises himself as an angel of light. [15] So it is no wonder that his servants also disguise themselves as servants of righteousness. In the end they will get the punishment their wicked deeds deserve.

6. **Luke 10:17-18:** [17] When the seventy-two disciples returned, they joyfully reported to him, "Lord, even the demons obey us when we use your name!" [18] "Yes," he told them, "I saw Satan fall from heaven like lightning!"

7. **1 John 3:8:** But when people keep on sinning, it shows that they belong to the devil, who has been sinning since the beginning. But the Son of God came to destroy the works of the devil.

8. **Colossians 1:13-14:** [13] For he has rescued us from the kingdom of darkness and transferred us into the Kingdom of his dear Son, [14] who purchased our freedom and forgave our sins.

9. **Zechariah 3:1-2:** Then the angel showed me Jeshua the high priest standing before the angel of the Lord. The Accuser, Satan, was there at the angel's right hand, making accusations against Jeshua. [2] And the Lord said to Satan, "I, the Lord, reject your accusations, Satan. Yes, the Lord, who has chosen Jerusalem, rebukes you. This man is like a burning stick that has been snatched from the fire."

10. **Revelation 12:10:** Then I heard a loud voice shouting across the heavens, "It has come at last, salvation and power and the Kingdom of our God, and the authority of his Christ. For the accuser of our brothers and sisters has been thrown down to earth, the one who accuses them before our God day and night."

11. **John 10:10:** The thief's purpose is to steal and kill and destroy. My purpose is to give them a rich and satisfying life.

12. **Genesis 3:1-24:** The serpent was the shrewdest of all the wild animals the Lord God had made. One day he asked the woman, "Did God really say you must not eat the fruit from any of the trees in the garden?"[2] "Of course we may eat fruit from the trees in the garden," the woman replied. [3] "It's only the fruit from the tree in the middle of the garden that we are not allowed to eat. God said, 'You must not eat it or even touch it; if you do, you will die.'" [4] "You won't die!" the serpent replied to the woman. [5] "God knows that your eyes will be opened as soon as you eat it, and you will be like God, knowing both good and evil." [6] The woman was convinced. She saw that the tree was beautiful and its fruit looked delicious, and she wanted the wisdom it would give her. So she took some of the fruit and ate it. Then she gave some to her husband, who was with her, and he ate it, too. [7] At that moment their eyes were opened, and they suddenly felt shame at their nakedness. So they sewed fig leaves together to cover themselves. [8] When the cool evening breezes were blowing, the man and his wife heard the Lord God walking about in the garden. So they hid from the Lord God among the trees. [9] Then the Lord God called to the man, "Where are you?" [10] He replied, "I heard you walking in the garden, so I hid. I was afraid because I was naked." [11] "Who told you that you were naked?" the Lord God asked. "Have you eaten from the tree whose fruit I commanded you not to eat?" [12] The man replied, "It was the woman you gave me who gave me the fruit, and I ate it." [13] Then the Lord God asked the woman, "What have you done?" "The serpent deceived me," she replied. "That's why I ate it." [14] Then the Lord God said to the serpent, "Because you have done this, you are cursed more than all animals, domestic and wild. You will crawl on

your belly, groveling in the dust as long as you live. [15] And I will cause hostility between you and the woman, and between your offspring and her offspring. He will strike your head, and you will strike his heel." [16] Then he said to the woman, "I will sharpen the pain of your pregnancy, and in pain you will give birth. And you will desire to control your husband, but he will rule over you." [17] And to the man he said, "Since you listened to your wife and ate from the tree whose fruit I commanded you not to eat, the ground is cursed because of you. All your life you will struggle to scratch a living from it. [18] It will grow thorns and thistles for you, though you will eat of its grains. [19] By the sweat of your brow will you have food to eat until you return to the ground from which you were made. For you were made from dust, and to dust you will return." [20] Then the man Adam named his wife Eve, because she would be the mother of all who live. [21] And the Lord God made clothing from animal skins for Adam and his wife. [22] Then the Lord God said, "Look, the human beings have become like us, knowing both good and evil. What if they reach out, take fruit from the tree of life, and eat it? Then they will live forever!" [23] So the Lord God banished them from the Garden of Eden, and he sent Adam out to cultivate the ground from which he had been made. [24] After sending them out, the Lord God stationed mighty cherubim to the east of the Garden of Eden. And he placed a flaming sword that flashed back and forth to guard the way to the tree of life.

13. **Job 1:1-12:** [6] One day the members of the heavenly court came to present themselves before the Lord, and the Accuser, Satan, came with them. [7] "Where have you come from?" the Lord asked Satan. Satan answered the Lord, "I have been patrolling the earth, watching everything that's going on." [8] Then the Lord asked Satan, "Have you noticed my servant Job? He is the finest man in all the earth. He is blameless, a man of complete integrity. He fears God and stays away from evil." [9] Satan replied to the Lord, "Yes, but Job has good reason to fear God. [10] You have always put a wall of protection around him and his home and his property. You have made him prosper in everything he does. Look how rich he is! [11] But reach out

and take away everything he has, and he will surely curse you to your face!" [12] "All right, you may test him," the Lord said to Satan. "Do whatever you want with everything he possesses, but don't harm him physically." So Satan left the Lord's presence.

14. **Luke 22:31-32:** [31] "Simon, Simon, Satan has asked to sift each of you like wheat. 32 But I have pleaded in prayer for you, Simon, that your faith should not fail. So when you have repented and turned to me again, strengthen your brothers."

15. **Luke 22:3:** Then Satan entered into Judas Iscariot, who was one of the twelve disciples..

16. **Acts 10:38:** And you know that God anointed Jesus of Nazareth with the Holy Spirit and with power. Then Jesus went around doing good and healing all who were oppressed by the devil, for God was with him.

17. **1 Thessalonians 2:18:** We wanted very much to come to you, and I, Paul, tried again and again, but Satan prevented us.

18. **1 Peter 5:8-9:** [8] Stay alert! Watch out for your great enemy, the devil. He prowls around like a roaring lion, looking for someone to devour. [9] Stand firm against him, and be strong in your faith. Remember that your family of believers all over the world is going through the same kind of suffering you are.

19. **2 Corinthians 12:7b:** ...even though I have received such wonderful revelations from God. So to keep me from becoming proud, I was given a thorn in my flesh, a messenger from Satan to torment me and keep me from becoming proud.

20. **Mark 5:1-15:** So they arrived at the other side of the lake, in the region of the Gerasenes [2] When Jesus climbed out of the boat, a man possessed by an evil spirit came out from the tombs to meet him. [3] This man lived in the burial caves and could no longer be restrained, even with a chain. [4] Whenever he was put into chains and shackles—as he often was—he snapped the chains from his wrists and smashed the shackles. No one was strong enough to subdue him. [5] Day and night he wandered among the burial caves and in the

hills, howling and cutting himself with sharp stones. [6] When Jesus was still some distance away, the man saw him, ran to meet him, and bowed low before him. [7] With a shriek, he screamed, "Why are you interfering with me, Jesus, Son of the Most High God? In the name of God, I beg you, don't torture me!" [8] For Jesus had already said to the spirit, "Come out of the man, you evil spirit."[9] Then Jesus demanded, "What is your name?" And he replied, "My name is Legion, because there are many of us inside this man." [10] Then the evil spirits begged him again and again not to send them to some distant place. [11] There happened to be a large herd of pigs feeding on the hillside nearby. [12] "Send us into those pigs," the spirits begged. "Let us enter them." [13] So Jesus gave them permission. The evil spirits came out of the man and entered the pigs, and the entire herd of about 2,000 pigs plunged down the steep hillside into the lake and drowned in the water. [14] The herdsmen fled to the nearby town and the surrounding countryside, spreading the news as they ran. People rushed out to see what had happened. [15] A crowd soon gathered around Jesus, and they saw the man who had been possessed by the legion of demons. He was sitting there fully clothed and perfectly sane, and they were all afraid.

21. **Luke 8:26-29:** [26] So they arrived in the region of the Gerasenes, across the lake from Galilee. [27] As Jesus was climbing out of the boat, a man who was possessed by demons came out to meet him. For a long time he had been homeless and naked, living in the tombs outside the town. [28] As soon as he saw Jesus, he shrieked and fell down in front of him. Then he screamed, "Why are you interfering with me, Jesus, Son of the Most High God? Please, I beg you, don't torture me!" [29] For Jesus had already commanded the evil spirit to come out of him. This spirit had often taken control of the man. Even when he was placed under guard and put in chains and shackles, he simply broke them and rushed out into the wilderness, completely under the demon's power.

22. **Luke 13:11:** ...he saw a woman who had been crippled by an evil spirit. She had been bent double for eighteen years and was unable to stand up straight.

23. **Matthew 12:22:** Then a demon-possessed man, who was blind and couldn't speak, was brought to Jesus. He healed the man so that he could both speak and see.

24. **Matthew 12:24:** But when the Pharisees heard about the miracle, they said, "No wonder he can cast out demons. He gets his power from Satan, the prince of demons."

25. **Daniel 10:13:** But for twenty-one days the spirit prince of the kingdom of Persia blocked my way. Then Michael, one of the archangels, came to help me, and I left him there with the spirit prince of the kingdom of Persia.

26. **Ephesians 6:10-12:** [10] A final word: Be strong in the Lord and in his mighty power. [11] Put on all of God's armor so that you will be able to stand firm against all strategies of the devil. [12] For we are not fighting against flesh-and-blood enemies, but against evil rulers and authorities of the unseen world, against mighty powers in this dark world, and against evil spirits in the heavenly places.

27. **Luke 4:5-6:** [5] Then the devil took him (Jesus) up and revealed to him all the kingdoms of the world in a moment of time. [6] "I will give you the glory of these kingdoms and authority over them," the devil said, "because they are mine to give to anyone I please."

28. **John 12:31:** The time for judging this world has come, when Satan, the ruler of this world, will be cast out.

29. **2 Corinthians 4:3-4:** [3] If the Good News we preach is hidden behind a veil, it is hidden only from people who are perishing. [4] Satan, who is the god of this world, has blinded the minds of those who don't believe. They are unable to see the glorious light of the Good News. They don't understand this message about the glory of Christ, who is the exact likeness of God.

30. **1 John 5:19:** We know that we are children of God and that the world around us is under the control of the evil one.

31. **Ephesians 2:1-2:** Once you were dead because of your disobedience and your many sins. [2] You used to live in sin, just like the rest of the world, obeying the devil - the commander of the powers in the unseen world. He is the spirit at work in the hearts of those who refuse to obey God.

32. **Joshua 24:15:** "But if you refuse to serve the Lord, then choose today whom you will serve. Would you prefer the gods your ancestors served beyond the Euphrates? Or will be the gods of the Amorites in whose land you now live? But as for me and my family, we will serve the Lord."

33. **2 Timothy 2:25-26:** [25] Gently instruct those who oppose the truth. Perhaps God will change those people's hearts, and they will learn the truth. [26] Then they will come to their senses and escape from the devil's trap. For they have been held captive by him to do whatever he wants.

34. **Matthew 12:30:** Jesus said "Anyone who isn't with me opposes me, and anyone who isn't working with me is actually working against me."

35. **1 John 3:9-10:** [9] Those who have been born into God's family do not make a practice of sinning, because God's life is in them. So they can't keep on sinning, because they are children of God. [10] So now we can tell who are children of God and who are children of the devil. Anyone who does not live righteously and does not love other believers does not belong to God.

36. **Acts 26:15-18:** [15] "'Who are you, lord?' I asked. "And the Lord replied, 'I am Jesus, the one you are persecuting. [16] Now get to your feet! For I have appeared to you to appoint you as my servant and witness. Tell people that you have seen me, and tell them what I will show you in the future. [17] And I will rescue you from both your own people and the Gentiles. Yes, I am sending you to the Gentiles [18] to open their eyes, so they may turn from darkness to light and from the power of

Satan to God. Then they will receive forgiveness for their sins and be given a place among God's people, who are set apart by faith in me.'

37. **Revelation 3:15-16:** [15] "I know all the things you do, that you are neither hot nor cold. I wish that you were one or the other! [16] But since you are like lukewarm water, neither hot nor cold, I will spit you out of my mouth!"

38. **Luke 8:12:** The seeds that fell on the footpath represent those who hear the message, only to have the devil come and take it away from their hearts and prevent them from believing and being saved.

39. **Jude 1:9:** But even Michael, one of the mightiest of the angels, did not dare accuse the devil of blasphemy, but simply said, "The Lord rebuke you!" (This took place when Michael was arguing with the devil about Moses' body.)

40. **Deuteronomy 18:9-14:** [9] "When you enter the land the Lord your God is giving you, be very careful not to imitate the detestable customs of the nations living there. [10] For example, never sacrifice your son or daughter as a burnt offering. And do not let your people practice fortune-telling, or use sorcery, or interpret omens, or engage in witchcraft, [11] or cast spells, or function as mediums or psychics, or call forth the spirits of the dead. [12] Anyone who does these things is detestable to the Lord. It is because the other nations have done these detestable things that the Lord your God will drive them out ahead of you. [13] But you must be blameless before the Lord your God. [14] The nations you are about to displace consult sorcerers and fortune-tellers, but the Lord your God forbids you to do such things."

41. **Isaiah 8:19:** Someone may say to you, "Let's ask the mediums and those who consult the spirits of the dead. With their whisperings and mutterings, they will tell us what to do." But shouldn't people ask God for guidance? Should the living seek guidance from the dead?"

42. **James 4:7:** So humble yourselves before God. Resist the devil, and he will flee from you.

43. **Ephesians 6:13-18:** [13] Therefore, put on every piece of God's armor so you will be able to resist the enemy in the time of evil. Then after

the battle you will still be standing firm. [14] Stand your ground, putting on the belt of truth and the body armor of God's right eousness. [15] For shoes, put on the peace that comes from the Good News so that you will be fully prepared. [16] In addition to all of these, hold up the shield of faith to stop the fiery arrows of the devil. [17] Put on salvation as your helmet, and take the sword of the Spirit, which is the word of God. [18] Pray in the Spirit at all times and on every occasion. Stay alert and be persistent in your prayers for all believers everywhere.

44. **2 Thessalonians 2:9-10:** [9] This man will come to do the work of Satan with counterfeit power and signs and miracles. [10] He will use every kind of evil deception to fool those on their way to destruction, because they refuse to love and accept the truth that would save them.

45. **Revelation 16:14:** [14] They are demonic spirits who work miracles and go out to all the rulers of the world to gather them for battle against the Lord on that great judgment day of God the Almighty.

46. **Revelation 19:20:** [20] And the beast was captured, and with him the false prophet who did mighty miracles on behalf of the beast— miracles that deceived all who had accepted the mark of the beast and who worshiped his statue. Both the beast and his false prophet were thrown alive into the fiery lake of burning sulfur.

47. **Revelation 13:11-15:** [11] Then I saw another beast come up out of the earth. He had two horns like those of a lamb, but he spoke with the voice of a dragon. [12] He exercised all the authority of the first beast. And he required all the earth and its people to worship the first beast, whose fatal wound had been healed. [13] He did astounding miracles, even making fire flash down to earth from the sky while everyone was watching. [14] And with all the miracles he was allowed to perform on behalf of the first beast, he deceived all the people who belong to this world. He ordered the people to make a great statue of the first beast, who was fatally wounded and then came back to life. [15] He was then permitted to give life to this statue so that

it could speak. Then the statue of the beast commanded that anyone refusing to worship it must die.

48. **Revelation 20:7-10:** [7] When the thousand years come to an end, Satan will be let out of his prison. [8] He will go out to deceive the nations, called Gog and Magog, in every corner of the earth. He will gather them together for battle—a mighty army, as numberless as sand along the seashore. [9] And I saw them as they went up on the broad plain of the earth and surrounded God's people and the beloved city. But fire from heaven came down on the attacking armies and consumed them. [10] Then the devil, who had deceived them, was thrown into the fiery lake of burning sulfur, joining the beast and the false prophet. There they will be tormented day and night forever and ever.

49. **Matthew 25:41:** [41] "Then the King will turn to those on the left and say, 'Away with you, you cursed ones, into the eternal fire prepared for the devil and his demons.'

50. **Proverbs 3:5-6:** [5] Trust in the Lord with all your heart; do not depend on your own understanding. [6] Seek his will in all you do, and he will show you which path to take.

51. **Proverbs 4:10-13:** [10] My child, listen to me and do as I say, and you will have a long, good life. [11] I will teach you wisdom's ways and lead you in straight paths. [12] When you walk, you won't be held back; when you run, you won't stumble. [13] Take hold of my instructions; don't let them go. Guard them, for they are the key to life.

CHAPTER TEN
BAPTISM

Baptism is a visible display of the spiritual change that takes place in our hearts after we receive salvation from the Lord Jesus Christ. There is usually a succession of events that take place leading up to baptism. Initially, we come to the realization that we have sinned against God and need His forgiveness. We then repent, which is a purposeful choice to turn *from* the direction our lives are headed, and turn *to* God. The next step we must take is to be baptized (Matthew 3:6[1]; Luke 3:3[2]).

Baptism is one of the few commands from the Lord to His followers, and it has deep spiritual significance. It is a *public sign of our inner repentance and willingness to love God* (Mark 1:4[3]). Baptism is symbolic of the "death", "burial", and "resurrection" that we experience as disciples of Jesus. This may sound morbid, but the Bible explains this process as the *rebirth*, literally being *born again.* In this light, we can see that baptism represents "dying" to our old life (immersion into the water), and being "raised" to our new life in Christ (coming up out of the water) (Romans 6:1-4[4]; 7:4[5]).

Sin and selfishness are so powerfully ingrained in us, that we need to 'put it to death' in order for us to receive the newness of life that Jesus offers (2 Corinthians 5:17[6]; Colossians 3:5[7]). Of course, even though we receive a different life from God, this doesn't mean that all of our choices from this point on will be perfect! Our old nature – the part of us that will always clash with God - will be with us until we are with the Lord in eternity.

However, new life is possible! When we are born again, God imparts to us the same power that raised Jesus from the dead – the power of God, the Holy Spirit (Acts 2:38[8]). We really *can* have new thoughts, feelings, actions, and speech, because as Christians, the Holy Spirit now lives within us. And we desperately need His strength in our lives, because we will constantly battle our old nature, outside influences, and the devil. Even Jesus was baptized *before* he was tempted by Satan in the desert (Mark 1:9-13[9]).

As we become one with Jesus through baptism, we will begin to develop the strength and the desire to *choose* good over evil, obedience over rebellion, and spiritual life over death (Galatians 3:27[10]). We will gain a deeper awareness, the capacity to fight sin, and the wisdom and power to do away with our old lifestyles. We will even be able to lose our fear of death (Hebrews 2:10-15[11]).

Additionally, we become "joint heirs" with Jesus, which means that all of God's promises to Christ now belong to us (Galatians 3:26-29[12]). There is a new hope for us, because we are now able to live a worthy life here on earth. As we are "crucified, buried, and resurrected" with Christ through baptism, we also obtain a *future* hope that we will receive our new resurrected bodies and live with Christ forever after we die (Romans 6:5-7[13]; 1 Thessalonians 5:10[14]).

We Are Family

The Bible says that as we receive Jesus into our hearts and are baptized, we are now the true children of God, connected and identified with Christ and His Church. Baptism proclaims to our new family – those who love Jesus - that we want our lives to be **united** with theirs (1 Corinthians 12:13[15]; Ephesians 4:1-6[16]).

This word *unite* in the Greek means "to bond" (cleave), "to adhere to" (literally, *glued together*); "to join to"; or "to become intimately connected in a soul-knit friendship". The church is now our *real* family, because a spiritual bond runs even deeper than a blood bond. That is why we can meet another Christian from any nation, tribe, or language, and feel a connection to them.

In fact, Jesus says that *only* the people who do the will of His Father are His legitimate family. This means that we will not spend eternity with our biological family *unless they have repented and committed their lives to Jesus* (Matthew 12:47-50[17]). In other words, the spiritual trumps the physical, and the only family we will spend eternity with in God's presence are other authentic disciples of Christ (1 Thessalonians 4:13-18[18]). May this inspire you to begin praying for your unsaved family members, and share Jesus with them.

Water or Sprinkling?

The original Greek word for *baptize* is "baptizo" which literally means "to make overwhelmed (i.e. fully wet); or "to cover wholly with a fluid". John the Baptizer frequently baptized people in the Jordan River, and he specifically baptized where there was plenty of water (John 3:23[19]). When Jesus, our Prime Example, was baptized, the Bible says "He came up *out of the water*" – meaning that He was fully submerged (Matthew 3:16-17[20]). Note that God was fully pleased with His Son during this event.

Some faiths believe that sprinkling water on a person or dipping them in water is baptism, but if that were so, John the Baptist could have baptized anywhere. Indeed, the Greek word for *sprinkle* is completely different than the one used for *baptize*. It is the word "rhantismos", which described the blood that was sprinkled on the Tabernacle in the Old Testament Temple (Hebrews 9:18-22[21]). (The book of Hebrews is Greek in origin, but it often refers back to the Old Testament). However, the "blood sprinkling/animal-sacrificing system" was done away with when Christ sacrificed His own blood for the purification of His people and the forgiveness of their sins (Hebrews 10:11-18[22]).

Lastly, some faiths believe in infant baptism (sprinkling). Yet there are no biblical accounts of *baptizing* an infant. Infants or children can be brought before the congregation to "dedicate" them to the Lord. The reason they aren't baptized at such an early age is because the Bible tells us that we are to repent and confess our faith in Christ preceding baptism.

This infers a certain level of maturity – what we call "an age of accountability", which usually begins around ages 8-10, depending on the child. Babies are born with a sin nature, for sure, but they are not able to *decide* to obey. Neither do they have the self-control not to sin – or to repent - until they are much older. This is why infant baptism is not found in the Bible.

I do understand that many people who were sprinkled as an infant, or were too ill to be immersed at their baptism, accept their baptism in their hearts. They confirm and acknowledge their baptism when they go through catechism or confirmation classes when they are at the age of accountability. My desire is not to create controversy. I am merely pointing out what is written about baptism in the Bible.

Obedience Is A Sign of Love

As we follow our Lord's directive in baptism, we display our love for Him. I like to think of obedience as a way of saying "Yes!" to Jesus, much as a bride says "yes" to her future husband. It is letting Jesus know that we are fully His, and that we want to shed our old life and embrace our new identity with God. We always benefit when we obey the Lord in the way He instructs us to.

Jesus tells us to "Take up our cross and follow Him" (Luke 9:23-24[23]). He wants us to be completely devoted to Him - to "Love the Lord with all your heart, mind, soul, and strength" (Deuteronomy 6:4-9[24]; Matthew 22:37-40[25]). He is delighted when we choose to love and obey Him regardless of the consequences.

Baptism is just another beautiful way to show
our commitment to Jesus

CHAPTER 10
Scripture Verses

1. **Matthew 3:6:** And when they confessed their sins, he baptized them in the Jordan River.

2. **Luke 3:3:** Then John went from place to place on both sides of the Jordan River, preaching that people should be baptized to show that they had repented of their sins and turned to God to be forgiven.

3. **Mark 1:4:** This messenger was John the Baptist. He was in the wilderness and preached that people should be baptized to show that they had repented of their sins and turned to God to be forgiven.

4. **Romans 6:1-4:** Well then, should we keep on sinning so that God can show us more and more of his wonderful grace? ² Of course not! Since we have died to sin, how can we continue to live in it? ³ Or have you forgotten that when we were joined with Christ Jesus in baptism, we joined him in his death? ⁴ For we died and were buried with Christ by baptism. And just as Christ was raised from the dead by the glorious power of the Father, now we also may live new lives.

5. **Romans 7:4:** So, my dear brothers and sisters, this is the point: You died to the power of the law when you died with Christ. And now you are united with the one who was raised from the dead. As a result, we can produce a harvest of good deeds for God.

6. **2 Corinthians 5:17:** This means that anyone who belongs to Christ has become a new person. The old life is gone; a new life has begun!

7. **Colossians 3:5:** So put to death the sinful, earthly things lurking within you. Have nothing to do with sexual immorality, impurity, lust, and evil desires. Don't be greedy, for a greedy person is an idolater, worshiping the things of this world.

8. **Acts 2:38:** Peter replied, "Each of you must repent of your sins and turn to God, and be baptized in the name of Jesus Christ for the

forgiveness of your sins. Then you will receive the gift of the Holy Spirit."

9. **Mark 1:9-13:** One day Jesus came from Nazareth in Galilee, and John baptized him in the Jordan River. [10] As Jesus came up out of the water, he saw the heavens splitting apart and the Holy Spirit descending on him like a dove. [11] And a voice from heaven said, "You are my dearly loved Son, and you bring me great joy." [12] The Spirit then compelled Jesus to go into the wilderness, [13] where he was tempted by Satan for forty days. He was out among the wild animals, and angels took care of him.

10. **Galatians 3:27:** And all who have been united with Christ in baptism have put on Christ, like putting on new clothes.

11. **Hebrews 2:10-15:** God, for whom and through whom everything was made, chose to bring many children into glory. And it was only right that he should make Jesus, through his suffering, a perfect leader, fit to bring them into their salvation. [11] So now Jesus and the ones he makes holy have the same Father. That is why Jesus is not ashamed to call them his brothers and sisters. [12] For he said to God, "I will proclaim your name to my brothers and sisters. I will praise you among your assembled people." [13] He also said, "I will put my trust in him," that is, "I and the children God has given me." [14] Because God's children are human beings - made of flesh and blood—the Son also became flesh and blood. For only as a human being could he die, and only by dying could he break the power of the devil, who had the power of death. [15] Only in this way could he set free all who have lived their lives as slaves to the fear of dying.

12. **Galatians 3:26-29:** For you are all children of God through faith in Christ Jesus. [27] And all who have been united with Christ in baptism have put on Christ, like putting on new clothes. [28] There is no longer Jew or Gentile, slave or free, male and female. For you are all one in Christ Jesus. [29] And now that you belong to Christ, you are the

true children of Abraham. You are his heirs, and God's promise to Abraham belongs to you.

13. **Romans 6:5-7:** Since we have been united with him in his death, we will also be raised to life as he was. [6] We know that our old sinful selves were crucified with Christ so that sin might lose its power in our lives. We are no longer slaves to sin. [7] For when we died with Christ we were set free from the power of sin.

14. **1 Thessalonians 5:10:** Christ died for us so that, whether we are dead or alive when he returns, we can live with him forever.

15. **1 Corinthians 12:13:** Some of us are Jews, some are Gentiles, some are slaves, and some are free. But we have all been baptized into one body by one Spirit, and we all share the same Spirit.

16. **Ephesians 4:1-6:** Therefore I, a prisoner for serving the Lord, beg you to lead a life worthy of your calling, for you have been called by God. [2] Always be humble and gentle. Be patient with each other, making allowance for each other's faults because of your love. [3] Make every effort to keep yourselves united in the Spirit, binding yourselves together with peace. [4] For there is one body and one Spirit, just as you have been called to one glorious hope for the future. [5] There is one Lord, one faith, one baptism, [6] one God and Father of all, who is over all, in all, and living through all.

17. **Matthew 12:47-50:** [47]Someone told Jesus, "Your mother and your brothers are standing outside, and they want to speak to you." [48] Jesus asked, "Who is my mother? Who are my brothers?" [49] Then he pointed to his disciples and said, "Look, these are my mother and brothers. [50] Anyone who does the will of my Father in heaven is my brother and sister and mother!"

18. **1 Thessalonians 4:13-18:** And now, dear brothers and sisters, we want you to know what will happen to the believers who have died so you will not grieve like people who have no hope. [14] For since we believe that Jesus died and was raised to life again, we also believe

that when Jesus returns, God will bring back with him the believers who have died. [15] We tell you this directly from the Lord: We who are still living when the Lord returns will not meet him ahead of those who have died. [16] For the Lord himself will come down from heaven with a commanding shout, with the voice of the archangel, and with the trumpet call of God. First, the believers who have died will rise from their graves. [17] Then, together with them, we who are still alive and remain on the earth will be caught up in the clouds to meet the Lord in the air. Then we will be with the Lord forever. [18] So encourage each other with these words.

19. **John 3:23:** At this time John the Baptist was baptizing at Aenon, near Salim, because there was plenty of water there; and people kept coming to him for baptism.

20. **Matthew 3:16-17:** After his baptism, as Jesus came up out of the water, the heavens were opened and he saw the Spirit of God descending like a dove and settling on him. [17] And a voice from heaven said, "This is my dearly loved Son, who brings me great joy."

21. **Hebrews 9:18-22:** That is why even the first covenant was put into effect with the blood of an animal. [19] For after Moses had read each of God's commandments to all the people, he took the blood of calves and goats, along with water, and sprinkled both the book of God's law and all the people, using hyssop branches and scarlet wool. [20] Then he said, "This blood confirms the covenant God has made with you." [21] And in the same way, he sprinkled blood on the Tabernacle and on everything used for worship. [22] In fact, according to the law of Moses, nearly everything was purified with blood. For without the shedding of blood, there is no forgiveness.

22. **Hebrews 10:11-18:** [11]Under the old covenant, the priest stands and ministers before the altar day after day, offering the same sacrifices again and again, which can never take away sins. [12] But our High Priest offered himself to God as a single sacrifice for sins, good for all time. Then he sat down in the place of honor at God's right hand. [13] There

he waits until his enemies are humbled and made a footstool under his feet. [14] For by that one offering he forever made perfect those who are being made holy. [15] And the Holy Spirit also testifies that this is so. For he says, [16] "This is the new covenant I will make with my people on that day, says the Lord: I will put my laws in their hearts, and I will write them on their minds." [17] Then he says, "I will never again remember their sins and lawless deeds." [18] And when sins have been forgiven, there is no need to offer any more sacrifices.

23. **Luke 9:23-24:** [23]Then he said to the crowd, "If any of you wants to be my follower, you must give up your own way, take up your cross daily, and follow me. [24] If you try to hang on to your life, you will lose it. But if you give up your life for my sake, you will save it."

24. **Deuteronomy 6:4-9:** [4]"Listen, O Israel! The Lord is our God, the Lord alone. [5] And you must love the Lord your God with all your heart, all your soul, and all your strength. [6] And you must commit yourselves wholeheartedly to these commands that I am giving you today. [7] Repeat them again and again to your children. Talk about them when you are at home and when you are on the road, when you are going to bed and when you are getting up. [8] Tie them to your hands and wear them on your forehead as reminders. [9] Write them on the doorposts of your house and on your gates."

25. **Matthew 22:37-40:** [37] Jesus replied, "'You must love the Lord your God with all your heart, all your soul, and all your mind.' [38] This is the first and greatest commandment. [39] A second is equally important: 'Love your neighbor as yourself.' [40] The entire law and all the demands of the prophets are based on these two commandments."

CHAPTER 11
TITHING

Money is probably one of the most difficult topics to talk about. It creates more anxiety than almost any other subject in life. Money practically tops the list of what people argue about, and it has destroyed countless relationships. So naturally, when God asks us to tithe - to return to Him a portion of our finances - we make excuses and become defensive! Why does money create such deep emotion in us?

Jesus spoke of money almost more than any other matter the Bible. He knew we would have a hard time sharing, giving, managing, and releasing our cash to Him and to others who are less fortunate than ourselves. This is because money represents our *blood, sweat, and tears.* Indeed, it is a reflection of the *life* we have poured out to make a living.

Money allows us to live more comfortably. It can give us a sense of security. But it can also be misused and overvalued. Any time we allow our *self-worth* to be attached to our assets, we are in danger, because money is so unpredictable. We can lose our wealth in an instant – due to sickness, injury, or catastrophe.

And that is exactly why God asks us to give Him a part of our finances. HE wants to become our comfort and our security, because He knows He is the only One who is absolutely stable in the universe. Everything except God *will* change. And more importantly, *He* wants to be the One to impart genuine worth and value to our lives.

What Is A Tithe?

The word *tithe* means "a tenth". It is a biblical directive that began early in the Old Testament (Genesis 28:22[1]). God Himself established the tithe so that His people would have a way to demonstrate their gratitude for all He had done for them (Numbers 18:25-29[2]). And the Israelites were to return to Him a portion of what He had already given them, so they would understand they were not self-sufficient.

Releasing a tenth of their best work and product back to the Lord was also a way to prevent the people from becoming proud and selfish. It taught them to respect God, because He literally owns heaven and earth and therefore, He deserves to be honored (Deuteronomy 14:22-23[3]; Leviticus 27:30[4]).

In the same way, the tithe benefits us in many ways today. The truth is, God doesn't need our money! But when we lovingly give to Him what we would rather cling to and hoard, we loosen the iron fist we tend to have on our finances. When we tithe, we essentially admit that all we have comes from God, that we trust in His provision, and that we realize He deserves the best "harvest" from our lives.

But I Don't WANT To!

I have spoken with people who attend church, read the Bible and pray – BUT – they refuse to tithe. The real attitude behind this rebellion towards God is *pride, fear, and/or greed*. People say "I don't have enough money to survive on – how am I supposed to give God any money"? They exclaim: "I made this money and I'm certainly not going to throw it away to the poor or to the church"! Or they may say, "Tithing is an Old Testament ritual and doesn't have anything to do with my circumstances today".

However, these are simply excuses to avoid doing what God has asked them to do. The Bible is clear about the consequences for obeying and disobeying – either we reap a positive or negative outcome from our choices. Make no mistake - God has much to say about the greedy person (Ephesians 5:5[5]; Colossians 3:5[6]; 2 Timothy 3:1-5[7]). In fact, greed is listed right up there with murder and hatred (Romans 1:29-32[8])!

In addition, people who refuse to tithe don't realize that it is truly a *joy* and a *freedom* to give God what He rightfully owns and deserves. Much of the fear we experience of losing or mismanaging our finances decreases when we handle our money according to God's design.

Tithes And Offerings

Jesus Himself tells us to tithe (Matthew 23:23[9]). The only difference between the Old and New Testament tithing is that our giving isn't as much about "the *tenth*" of our money, as it is "a proportion" of our money. If you have much, you give much. If you have little, you give less (2 Corinthians 8:1-15[10]). Your tithe can be a weekly or monthly practice, as you prefer.

Furthermore, it is not only biblical to tithe, but it's logical. The church and its workers need finances to operate! Additionally, it is God's plan that His people provide for those who minister and work for His Kingdom (1 Corinthians 9:13-14[11]; Galatians 6:6[12]).

Personally, the main reason I tithe is because I love Jesus. It's my honor and privilege to give back to Him what He has so generously given to me – which is much more than material blessings. Besides, the Bible tells us that the attitude in which we give is as significant to God as the money itself (2 Corinthians 9:5-15[13]). God delights in a cheerful giver!

An *offering* is a gift given apart from the tithe. It can be given any time there is an additional need in the church, or whenever the Lord directs you to help someone. This is the extra money that I give to missionaries, to the poor, and to other believers who may be struggling (Deuteronomy 16:9-10[14]).

As I trust God more fully, I find myself becoming more generous. And He has never let me down. I have reaped enormous benefits from lovingly obeying God in this matter. Joy, peace, and satisfaction are mine when I loosen my control over my finances. I don't "give to get", but in God's economy, we are sure to reap something of goodness when we live life the way He wants us to.

The bottom line is this: our tithes and offerings need to be given in a spirit of love and care in order to really honor the Lord. The truth is, He doesn't want our money if it's given spitefully, begrudgingly, or out of obligation (Luke 11:42[15]). And He doesn't want our "leftovers" – He wants the best we can give (Deuteronomy 17:1[16]).

God's Principles Of Giving And Receiving

The Bible tells us that God's ways and thoughts are far above our own (Isaiah 55:8-9[17]). His morals and values are pure. Therefore, His way of doing things often seem so contrary to what we think is right (Proverbs 16:25[18]). Nowhere do we see this more evident than in our giving. When God asks us to give, especially when it doesn't seem like we *have* anything to give, it can feel utterly foolish at times! But only when we follow His leading will we experience this crazy "joy" the Bible tells us we will experience if we unselfishly give (Acts 20:33-35[19]).

Our "heart" – our core intentions - determines what we say, do, and think. Jesus says "What you say flows from what is in your heart" (Luke 6:45[20]). Likewise, the true sign of our inner condition is reflected by the desire and ability we demonstrate when we unselfishly help others and honor God. Our heart motivation is the most important aspect of our lives, and it's what our Lord is most concerned with (Proverbs 4:23[21]; Matthew 15:16-20[22]).

I often say "If you do it God's way, you'll get *God's* results. If you do it your way, you'll get *your* results". I have found countless times that the outcome of "my ways" has disappointed me! There are untold individuals who have come to experience joy, peace, and contentment, because they have deliberately turned from their own ways, and have chosen to follow the Lord's direction.

When we love and trust God fully, we will naturally obey Him and serve Him by serving others. When we become generous with our time, talent, and treasure, we will experience great joy and favor (Psalm 112[23]). Now this doesn't mean that we will get rich if we are generous! However, our focus will change from being self-centered to other-centered.

Many times, we will receive peace and satisfaction as our reward for giving ourselves away. And don't underestimate the tremendous power of our heavenly reward, for it will be more splendid than anything we can imagine! This generous way of living is God's grand design for us, and He will honor a life such as this (Luke 6:38[24]).

On the contrary, being stingy with our money brings nothing but heartache (Proverbs 1:19[25]; 2 Peter 2:19[26]). You have probably heard the saying that money is evil, but the Bible actually says "The *love of money* is the root of all kinds of evil" (Ecclesiastes 5:10-11[27]; 1 Timothy 6:6-10[28]). Money itself is neutral, but the *affection* we place on it is what has the ability to make it so dangerous and damaging. This is the type of slavery God wants us to avoid. Indeed, God is a giver, and He loves it when we freely give of ourselves and our finances.

There is great freedom and joy in being a cheerful and generous giver!

CHAPTER 11
Scripture Verses

1. **Genesis 28:22:** "And this memorial pillar I have set up will become a place for worshiping God, and I will present to God a tenth of everything he gives me."

2. **Numbers 18:25-29:** [25] The Lord also told Moses, [26] "Give these instructions to the Levites: When you receive from the people of Israel the tithes I have assigned as your allotment, give a tenth of the tithes you receive—a tithe of the tithe—to the Lord as a sacred offering. [27] The Lord will consider this offering to be your harvest offering, as though it were the first grain from your own threshing floor or wine from your own winepress. [28] You must present one-tenth of the tithe received from the Israelites as a sacred offering to the Lord. This is the Lord's sacred portion, and you must present it to Aaron the priest. [29] Be sure to give to the Lord the best portions of the gifts given to you."

3. **Deuteronomy 14:22-23:** [22] "You must set aside a tithe of your crops - one-tenth of all the crops you harvest each year. [23] Bring this tithe to the designated place of worship - the place the Lord your God chooses for his name to be honored- and eat it there in his presence. This applies to your tithes of grain, new wine, olive oil, and the firstborn males of your flocks and herds. Doing this will teach you always to fear the Lord your God."

4. **Leviticus 27:30:** "One-tenth of the produce of the land, whether grain from the fields or fruit from the trees, belongs to the Lord and must be set apart to him as holy."

5. **Ephesians 5:5:** You can be sure that no immoral, impure, or greedy person will inherit the Kingdom of Christ and of God. For a greedy person is an idolater, worshiping the things of this world.

6. **Colossians 3:5:** [5] So put to death the sinful, earthly things lurking within you. Have nothing to do with sexual immorality, impurity, lust,

and evil desires. Don't be greedy, for a greedy person is an idolater, worshiping the things of this world.

7. **2 Timothy 3:1-5:** You should know this, Timothy, that in the last days there will be very difficult times. [2] For people will love only themselves and their money. They will be boastful and proud, scoffing at God, disobedient to their parents, and ungrateful. They will consider nothing sacred. [3] They will be unloving and unforgiving; they will slander others and have no self-control. They will be cruel and hate what is good. [4] They will betray their friends, be reckless, be puffed up with pride, and love pleasure rather than God. [5] They will act religious, but they will reject the power that could make them godly. Stay away from people like that!

8. **Romans 1:29-32:** [29] Their lives became full of every kind of wickedness, sin, greed, hate, envy, murder, quarreling, deception, malicious behavior, and gossip. [30] They are backstabbers, haters of God, insolent, proud, and boastful. They invent new ways of sinning, and they disobey their parents. [31] They refuse to understand, break their promises, are heartless, and have no mercy. [32] They know God's justice requires that those who do these things deserve to die, yet they do them anyway. Worse yet, they encourage others to do them, too.

9. **Matthew 23:23:** "What sorrow awaits you teachers of religious law and you Pharisees. Hypocrites! For you are careful to tithe even the tiniest income from your herb gardens, but you ignore the more important aspects of the law—justice, mercy, and faith. You should tithe, yes, but do not neglect the more important things."

10. **2 Corinthians 8:1-15:** Now I want you to know, dear brothers and sisters, what God in his kindness has done through the churches in Macedonia. [2] They are being tested by many troubles, and they are very poor. But they are also filled with abundant joy, which has overflowed in rich generosity. [3] For I can testify that they gave not only what they could afford, but far more. And they did it of their own free will. [4] They begged us again and again for the privilege of sharing in

the gift for the believers in Jerusalem. ⁵ They even did more than we had hoped, for their first action was to give themselves to the Lord and to us, just as God wanted them to do. ⁶ So we have urged Titus, who encouraged your giving in the first place, to return to you and encourage you to finish this ministry of giving. ⁷ Since you excel in so many ways—in your faith, your gifted speakers, your knowledge, your enthusiasm, and your love for us -I want you to excel also in this gracious act of giving. ⁸ I am not commanding you to do this. But I am testing how genuine your love is by comparing it with the eagerness of the other churches. ⁹ You know the generous grace of our Lord Jesus Christ. Though he was rich, yet for your sakes he became poor, so that by his poverty he could make you rich. ¹⁰ Here is my advice: It would be good for you to finish what you started a year ago. Last year you were the first who wanted to give, and you were the first to begin doing it. ¹¹ Now you should finish what you started. Let the eagerness you showed in the beginning be matched now by your giving. Give in proportion to what you have. ¹² Whatever you give is acceptable if you give it eagerly. And give according to what you have, not what you don't have. ¹³ Of course, I don't mean your giving should make life easy for others and hard for yourselves. I only mean that there should be some equality. ¹⁴ Right now you have plenty and can help those who are in need. Later, they will have plenty and can share with you when you need it. In this way, things will be equal. ¹⁵ As the Scriptures say, "Those who gathered a lot had nothing left over, and those who gathered only a little had enough."

11. **1 Corinthians 9:13-14:** ¹³ Don't you realize that those who work in the temple get their meals from the offerings brought to the temple? And those who serve at the altar get a share of the sacrificial offerings. ¹⁴ In the same way, the Lord ordered that those who preach the Good News should be supported by those who benefit from it.

12. **Galatians 6:6:** Those who are taught the word of God should provide for their teachers, sharing all good things with them.

13. **2 Corinthians 9:5-15:** ⁵ So I thought I should send these brothers ahead of me to make sure the gift you promised is ready. But I

want it to be a willing gift, not one given grudgingly. [6] Remember this - a farmer who plants only a few seeds will get a small crop. But the one who plants generously will get a generous crop. [7] You must each decide in your heart how much to give. And don't give reluctantly or in response to pressure. "For God loves a person who gives cheerfully." [8] And God will generously provide all you need. Then you will always have everything you need and plenty left over to share with others. [9] As the Scriptures say, "They share freely and give generously to the poor. Their good deeds will be remembered forever." [10] For God is the one who provides seed for the farmer and then bread to eat. In the same way, he will provide and increase your resources and then produce a great harvest of generosity in you. [11] Yes, you will be enriched in every way so that you can always be generous. And when we take your gifts to those who need them, they will thank God. [12] So two good things will result from this ministry of giving – the needs of the believers in Jerusalem will be met, and they will joyfully express their thanks to God. [13] As a result of your ministry, they will give glory to God. For your generosity to them and to all believers will prove that you are obedient to the Good News of Christ. [14] And they will pray for you with deep affection because of the overflowing grace God has given to you. [15] Thank God for this gift too wonderful for words!

14. **Deuteronomy 16:9-10:** [9] "Count off seven weeks from when you first begin to cut the grain at the time of harvest. [10] Then celebrate the Festival of Harvest to honor the Lord your God. Bring him a voluntary offering in proportion to the blessings you have received from him."

15. **Luke 11:42:** "What sorrow awaits you Pharisees! For you are careful to tithe even the tiniest income from your herb gardens, but you ignore justice and the love of God. You should tithe, yes, but do not neglect the more important things."

16. **Deuteronomy 17:1:** "Never sacrifice sick or defective cattle, sheep, or goats to the Lord your God, for he detests such gifts."

17. **Isaiah 55:8-9:** [8] "My thoughts are nothing like your thoughts," says the Lord. "And my ways are far beyond anything you could imagine. [9] For just as the heavens are higher than the earth, so my ways are higher than your ways and my thoughts higher than your thoughts."

18. **Proverbs 16:25:** There is a path before each person that seems right, but it ends in death.

19. **Acts 20:33-35:** [33] "I have never coveted anyone's silver or gold or fine clothes. [34] You know that these hands of mine have worked to supply my own needs and even the needs of those who were with me. [35] And I have been a constant example of how you can help those in need by working hard. You should remember the words of the Lord Jesus: 'It is more blessed to give than to receive.'"

20. **Luke 6:45:** A good person produces good things from the treasury of a good heart, and an evil person produces evil things from the treasury of an evil heart. What you say flows from what is in your heart.

21. **Proverbs 4:23:** Guard your heart above all else, for it determines the course of your life.

22. **Matthew 15:16-20:** [16] "Don't you understand yet?" Jesus asked. [17] "Anything you eat passes through the stomach and then goes into the sewer. [18] But the words you speak come from the heart - that's what defiles you. [19] For from the heart come evil thoughts, murder, adultery, all sexual immorality, theft, lying, and slander. [20] These are what defile you. Eating with unwashed hands will never defile you."

23. **Psalm 112:** [1] Praise the Lord! How joyful are those who fear the Lord and delight in obeying his commands. [2] Their children will be successful everywhere; an entire generation of godly people will be blessed. [3] They themselves will be wealthy, and their good deeds will last forever. [4] Light shines in the darkness for the godly. They are generous, compassionate, and righteous. [5] Good comes to those who lend money generously and conduct their business fairly. [6] Such people will not be overcome by evil. Those who are righteous will be long remembered. [7] They do not fear bad news; they confidently trust

the Lord to care for them. [8] They are confident and fearless and can face their foes triumphantly. [9] They share freely and give generously to those in need. Their good deeds will be remembered forever. They will have influence and honor. [10] The wicked will see this and be infuriated. They will grind their teeth in anger; they will slink away, their hopes thwarted.

24. **Luke 6:38:** Give, and you will receive. Your gift will return to you in full -pressed down, shaken together to make room for more, running over, and poured into your lap. The amount you give will determine the amount you get back.

25. **Proverbs 1:19:** Such is the fate of all who are greedy for money; it robs them of life.

26. **2 Peter 2:19:** They promise freedom, but they themselves are slaves of sin and corruption. For you are a slave to whatever controls you.

27. **Ecclesiastes 5:10-11:** [10] Those who love money will never have enough. How meaningless to think that wealth brings true happiness! [11] The more you have, the more people come to help you spend it. So what good is wealth - except perhaps to watch it slip through your fingers!

28. **1 Timothy 6:6-10:** [6] Yet true godliness with contentment is itself great wealth. [7] After all, we brought nothing with us when we came into the world, and we can't take anything with us when we leave it. [8] So if we have enough food and clothing, let us be content. [9] But people who long to be rich fall into temptation and are trapped by many foolish and harmful desires that plunge them into ruin and destruction. [10] For the love of money is the root of all kinds of evil. And some people, craving money, have wandered from the true faith and pierced themselves with many sorrows.

CHAPTER 12

COMMUNION

Most people have heard the word "communion" and may think of it as something that is "done in church" with a wafer and some wine or grape juice. This is an accurate description. But the reality behind the practice of communion is a very beautiful picture of God imparting His character into those who have received salvation from Jesus Christ.

The word *communion* comes from the Greek word *koinonia*, which means "to share in common". This can signify the sharing of thoughts, feelings, or customs. The actual word *communion* only appears in the King James Version of the Bible, and only 4 times in the New Testament. *Koinonia* can otherwise be translated as "fellowship", "partnership", or "partaker" (one who participates, shares, or joins in).

<u>Biblical Communion</u>

The New Testament teaches that Jesus directed His disciples to observe communion regularly (1 Corinthians 11:23-26[1]). On the very night He was betrayed – right before His crucifixion - He spoke the lasting words by which He wanted His followers to remember Him. The meal Jesus shared with them is referred to as "The Last Supper", because it was the final meal He ate with them. Nearing the end of the supper, Jesus broke the bread and offered it and the wine to His beloved friends.

He explained that the bread was symbolic of His body that was to be broken on the Cross, as He took upon Himself the sin of the world. The cup was to be a symbol of His blood that would be shed for them, and for the future generations of His followers. His blood was spilled to forgive us, cleanse us, and wash us from our sin.

Communion is also referred to as "The Lord's Supper" (Acts 2:42-47[2]). Jesus instructed these men to continue to share the bread and wine after His death, whenever they gathered (Luke 22:14-20[3]). He said that when they received the elements (bread and wine), it was to be a reminder of His sacrifice, which established the "New Covenant".

The "New Covenant" was foretold in the Old Testament hundreds of years before Christ came. This covenant, or promise, is Jesus' Once-and-for-all blood sacrifice for the forgiveness of sins. As we are pardoned and saved by the Lord Jesus, His Holy Spirit perfects our own communion, or relationship, with God (Jeremiah 31:33-34[4]; 2 Corinthians 3:3-11[5]).

Remember, the Old Covenant was the sacrificial system of blood of bulls and lambs, and had to be performed day after day, year after year. However, this entire system was but a foreshadow of Christ's Glorious Sacrifice – His very own death so that people who chose to believe in Him could be forgiven and reconciled to God. With the advent of our Lord, the old system was no longer needed and was abolished.

The Passover Meal

It is very interesting that Jesus called communion "The *Passover Meal*" in Luke 22:15[6]. The Old Testament Passover took place centuries before the birth of Jesus. The story tells of the Jews as they were about to leave Egypt, where they had been enslaved for 400 years. However, God was about to free them and bring them into the "Promised Land". This "land" is actually the country of Israel and the surrounding area today.

Incidentally, I like to relate this story of the Jews' freedom from bondage to the freedom *we* receive when we accept Jesus' payment for our sins. And just as they came into their Promised Land, I believe that for the Christian, the "Promised Land" is an intimate relationship with God now, as well as our future life with Him in eternity.

The Passover story tells us that Pharaoh, the king of Egypt, was having a hard time letting his Hebrew slaves go. God intervened by sending plague after plague to force him to release the Jews from his rule. The last adversity God inflicted was that of the Angel of Death. The Angel was sent to kill every firstborn son and male animal in the region (Exodus 12:11-13[7]). Interestingly, the book of Exodus is so named because it means "to leave".

Now, God wanted to protect His own people, so He instructed the Israelites to slaughter a lamb and paint its blood over the doorpost of their house. As the Angel of Death neared the homes that were "painted", he would "pass over", or spare, the firstborn son and animal of that house. Thus, the name "Passover".

Additionally, the Jews were to eat a meal of lamb and bread before they started their journey. The bread was to be unleavened (meaning no yeast was added to the bread), because they didn't have time to wait for it to rise. They were to be prepared to leave at a moment's notice.

This all is extremely significant as it relates to Jesus. First, He **is** the male Lamb, the Perfect Sacrifice (John 1:29-30[8]). Jesus offered His own blood, which symbolically "covers the doorpost" of the believer's life, and judgment is now *passed over* in our lives. Because of this amazing gift, the Christian is now spared spiritual death and eternal separation from God.

Furthermore, the Jews ate the Passover Meal *before the suffering began*, just as Jesus did (see Luke 22:15b[9] again). And just as God's people in the Exodus story were to be ready to leave at a moment's notice, we are to be ready at all times in anticipation of our Lord's return (1 Thessalonians 5:2[10]).

Motive For Communion

Now that we understand what communion is, we will turn to the importance of taking it seriously. The Bible says we can actually bring harm on ourselves if we take communion lightly or without repentance (1 Corinthians 11:27-32[11]). This section of Scripture is addressing the Corinthians' practice of using the bread and wine in their communion service to fill their bellies and get drunk!

It's unlikely that we will take communion for these reasons. But it is also a warning for *us* not to take communion if we have not confessed and repented of sin in our lives before we take of the elements. We are not to thoughtlessly commune with God! We are told to examine our inner hearts and outer actions to make sure we are right with God before we eat and drink the Lord's Supper (Hebrews 10:29[12]). As Christians, we have been bought with a precious and expensive price. Therefore, let us not take lightly that which has been so lovingly and sacrificially given (1 Peter 1:18-20[13]).

As time passes in our Christian life, we can begin to unintentionally make Jesus and His directives more of a ritual or a habit than a vital, dynamic way of life. When our faith becomes stale, loveless, or powerless – but we continue to "go through the motions" – this is basically called *religion*. Jesus detests religion! He wants to have a living, growing, exciting relationship with us. We need to guard this love connection every single day, and make intentional choices that will help us cultivate our union with Him.

Living for Jesus *can be* the most thrilling experience you can even imagine! But it takes time and effort to maintain. I pray this book has helped you understand the basic truths of the Christian life. I pray you will receive power from the Holy Spirit to live a life that pleases the Lord Jesus Christ. And I pray that you will completely surrender your life to Him. Life will always have its difficulties, but when you make Jesus your highest priority, you will be able to overcome and thrive in ways you never thought possible.

Strive to make Jesus your priority every day!

If you have remaining time after this last class, you can take time to share with your group the things you have learned from these studies. Write down some ways you can begin to love and serve Jesus more fully today.

Sharon ☺

CHAPTER 12
Scripture Verses

1. **1 Corinthians 11:23-26:** [23] For I pass on to you what I received from the Lord himself. On the night when he was betrayed, the Lord Jesus took some bread [24] and gave thanks to God for it. Then he broke it in pieces and said, "This is my body, which is given for you. Do this in remembrance of me." [25] In the same way, he took the cup of wine after supper, saying, "This cup is the new covenant between God and his people - an agreement confirmed with my blood. Do this in remembrance of me as often as you drink it." [26] For every time you eat this bread and drink this cup, you are announcing the Lord's death until he comes again.

2. **Acts 2:42-47:** [42] All the believers devoted themselves to the apostles' teaching, and to fellowship, and to sharing in meals (including the Lord's Supper), and to prayer. [43] A deep sense of awe came over them all, and the apostles performed many miraculous signs and wonders. [44] And all the believers met together in one place and shared everything they had. [45] They sold their property and possessions and shared the money with those in need. [46] They worshiped together at the Temple each day, met in homes for the Lord's Supper, and shared their meals with great joy and generosity - [47] all the while praising God and enjoying the goodwill of all the people. And each day the Lord added to their fellowship those who were being saved.

3. **Luke 22:14-20:** [14] When the time came, Jesus and the apostles sat down together at the table. [15] Jesus said, "I have been very eager to eat this Passover meal with you before my suffering begins. [16] For I tell you now that I won't eat this meal again until its meaning is fulfilled in the Kingdom of God." [17] Then he took a cup of wine and gave thanks to God for it. Then he said, "Take this and share it among yourselves. [18] For I will not drink wine again until the Kingdom of God has come." [19] He took some bread and gave thanks to God for it. Then he broke it in pieces and gave it to the disciples, saying, "This is my body, which is given for you. Do this in remembrance of

me."[20] After supper he took another cup of wine and said, "This cup is the new covenant between God and his people—an agreement confirmed with my blood, which is poured out as a sacrifice for you."

4. **Jeremiah 31:33-34:** [33] "But this is the new covenant I will make with the people of Israel after those days," says the Lord. "I will put my instructions deep within them, and I will write them on their hearts. I will be their God, and they will be my people. [34] And they will not need to teach their neighbors, nor will they need to teach their relatives, saying, 'You should know the Lord.' For everyone, from the least to the greatest, will know me already," says the Lord. "And I will forgive their wickedness, and I will never again remember their sins."

5. **2 Corinthians 3:3-11:** [3] Clearly, you are a letter from Christ showing the result of our ministry among you. This "letter" is written not with pen and ink, but with the Spirit of the living God. It is carved not on tablets of stone, but on human hearts. [4] We are confident of all this because of our great trust in God through Christ. [5] It is not that we think we are qualified to do anything on our own. Our qualification comes from God. [6] He has enabled us to be ministers of his new covenant. This is a covenant not of written laws, but of the Spirit. The old written covenant ends in death; but under the new covenant, the Spirit gives life.

The Glory of the New Covenant: [7] The old way, with laws etched in stone, led to death, though it began with such glory that the people of Israel could not bear to look at Moses' face. For his face shone with the glory of God, even though the brightness was already fading away. [8] Shouldn't we expect far greater glory under the new way, now that the Holy Spirit is giving life? [9] If the old way, which brings condemnation, was glorious, how much more glorious is the new way, which makes us right with God! [10] In fact, that first glory was not glorious at all compared with the overwhelming glory of the new way. [11] So if the old way, which has been replaced, was glorious, how much more glorious is the new, which remains forever!

6. **Luke 22:15:** Jesus said, "I have been very eager to eat this Passover meal with you before my suffering begins."

7. **Exodus 12:11-13:** [11] "These are your instructions for eating this meal: Be fully dressed, wear your sandals, and carry your walking stick in your hand. Eat the meal with urgency, for this is the Lord's Passover. [12] On that night I will pass through the land of Egypt and strike down every firstborn son and firstborn male animal in the land of Egypt. I will execute judgment against all the gods of Egypt, for I am the Lord! [13] But the blood on your doorposts will serve as a sign, marking the houses where you are staying. When I see the blood, I will pass over you. This plague of death will not touch you when I strike the land of Egypt.

8. **John 1:29-30:** [29] The next day John saw Jesus coming toward him and said, "Look! The Lamb of God who takes away the sin of the world! [30] He is the one I was talking about when I said, 'A man is coming after me who is far greater than I am, for he existed long before me.'

9. **Luke 22:15b:** Jesus said, "I have been very eager to eat this Passover meal with you **before my suffering begins**."

10. **1 Thessalonians 5:2:** For you know quite well that the day of the Lord's return will come unexpectedly, like a thief in the night.

11. **1 Corinthians 11:27-32:** [27] So anyone who eats this bread or drinks this cup of the Lord unworthily is guilty of sinning against the body and blood of the Lord. [28] That is why you should examine yourself before eating the bread and drinking the cup. [29] For if you eat the bread or drink the cup without honoring the body of Christ, you are eating and drinking God's judgment upon yourself. [30] That is why many of you are weak and sick and some have even died. [31] But if we would examine ourselves, we would not be judged by God in this way. [32] Yet when we are judged by the Lord, we are being disciplined so that we will not be condemned along with the world.

12. **Hebrews 10:29:** [29] Just think how much worse the punishment will be for those who have trampled on the Son of God, and have treated the blood of the covenant, which made us holy, as if it were common

and unholy, and have insulted and disdained the Holy Spirit, who brings God's mercy to us.

13. **1 Peter 1:18-20:** [18] For you know that God paid a ransom to save you from the empty life you inherited from your ancestors. And it was not paid with mere gold or silver, which lose their value. [19] It was the precious blood of Christ, the sinless, spotless Lamb of God. [20] God chose him as your ransom long before the world began, but now in these last days, he has been revealed for your sake.

Made in the USA
San Bernardino, CA
21 July 2018